98 97 96 95 94   5 4 3 2 1

Library of Congress Cataloging in Publication Data

Bova, Ben
    The craft of writing science fiction that sells / by Ben Bova.
        p.   cm.
    Includes bibliographical references.
    ISBN 0-89879-600-8
    1. Science fiction—Authorship. I. Title.
PN3377.5.S3B59   1993
808.3'8762—dc20   93-38613
                                                                 CIP

Edited by William Brohaugh
Designed by Clare Finney

THE CRAFT OF
WRITING
SCIENCE
FICTION
THAT SELLS

∎

BEN BOVA
Author of Mars and Millenium

WRITER'S DIGEST BOOKS

Cincinnati, Ohio

To Barbara and Bill, two of the most persistent people I know.

I shall always feel respect for every one who has written a book,
let it be what it may, for I had no idea of the trouble,
which trying to write common English could cost one.
—Charles Darwin

ABOUT THE AUTHOR

Ben Bova, author of more than eighty futuristic novels and non-fiction books, has been involved in science and high technology since the beginning of the space program. Formerly president of Science-fiction and Fantasy Writers of America and President Emeritus of the National Space Society, Bova is a frequent commentator on radio and television, and a popular lecturer. He has also been an editor and an executive in the aerospace industry.

His novels, such as *Mars* and *The Trikon Deception*, combine romance, adventure, and scientific accuracy to explore the impact of technological developments on individuals and on society as a whole. His nonfiction books, such as *Welcome to Moonbase* and *Assured Survival*, show how modern technology can be used to solve economic, social and political problems.

Bova has taught science fiction writing at Harvard University and at the Hayden Planetarium in New York City. He lectures regularly on topics dealing with the space program, energy, the craft of writing, and the art of predicting the future. His audiences have included the National Geographic Society, government and corporate executive groups, writers' workshops and university students. He has worked with film makers and television producers, such as Woody Allen, George Lucas and Gene Roddenberry.

Bova has appeared on hundreds of radio and television broadcasts. He was a regular guest on *CBS Morning News*, and has appeared frequently on *Good Morning America* and the *Today* show.

He was editorial director of *Omni* magazine and editor of *Analog* magazine. He received the Science Fiction Achievement Award (the "Hugo") for Best Professional Editor six times.

CONTENTS

Plot in Science Fiction

Chapter One

How to Get Out of the Slushpile

All good books are alike in that they are truer than if they had really happened and after you are finished reading one you will feel that all that happened to you and afterwards it all belongs to you; the good and the bad, the ecstasy, the remorse and sorrow, the people and the places and how the weather was. If you can get so that you can give that to people, then you are a writer.

—*Ernest Hemingway*

All my life I have been a writer.

Well, almost. As far back as I can remember I was writing stories or telling them to friends and family. When I was in junior high school I created a comic strip—strictly for myself; I had no thought of trying to publish it. And I enjoyed reading, enjoyed it immensely. Back in those days, when I was borrowing all the books I was allowed to from the South Philadelphia branch of the Free Library of Philadelphia, I had no way of knowing that every career in writing begins with a love of reading.

It was in South Philadelphia High School for Boys (back in those sexually segregated days) that I encountered Mr. George Paravicini, the tenth-grade English teacher and faculty advisor for the school newspaper, *The Southron*. Under his patient guidance, I worked on the paper and began to write fiction, as well.

Upon graduation from high school in 1949, the group of us who had produced the school paper for three years and published a spiffy yearbook for our graduating class decided that we would go into the magazine business. We created the nation's first magazine for teenagers, *Campus Town*. It was a huge success and a total failure. We published three issues, they were all immediate sellouts, yet somehow we went broke. That convinced us that we probably needed to know more than we did, and we went our separate ways to college.

While I was a staff editor of *Campus Town* I had my first fiction published. I wrote a short story for each of those three issues. I also had a story accepted by another Philadelphia magazine, for the princely payment of five dollars, but the magazine went bankrupt before they could publish it.

I worked my way through Temple University, getting a degree in journalism in 1954, then took a reporter's job on a suburban Philadelphia weekly newspaper, *The Upper Darby News*.

I was still writing fiction, but without much success. Like most fledgling writers, I had to work at a nine-to-five job to buy groceries and pay the rent. I moved from newspapers to aerospace and actually worked on the first U.S. space project, Vanguard, two years before the creation of NASA. Eventually, I became manager of marketing for a high-powered research lab in Massachusetts, the Avco Everett Research Laboratory. In that role I set up the first top-secret meeting in the Pentagon to inform the Department of Defense that we had invented high-power lasers. That was in 1966, and it was the beginning of what is now called the Strategic Defense Initiative, or Star Wars.

My first novel was published in 1959, and I began to have some success as a writer, although still not enough success to leave Avco and become a full-time writer. By then I had a wife and two children.

I became an editor by accident. John W. Campbell, the most powerful and influential editor in the science fiction field, died unexpectedly. I was asked to take his place as editor of *Analog Science Fiction-Science Fact* magazine, at that time (1971) the top magazine in the SF field. I spent the next eleven years in New York City, as editor of *Analog* and, later, *Omni* magazine.

In 1982 I left magazine editing. I have been a full-time writer and occasional lecturer ever since. I have written more than eighty fiction and nonfiction books, a hatful of short stories, and hundreds of articles, reviews and opinion pieces.

THE SLUSHPILE

When I was an editor of fiction, every week I received some fifty to a hundred story manuscripts from men and women who had never submitted a piece of fiction before. The manuscripts stacked up on my desk daily and formed what is known in the publishing business as "the slushpile." Every new writer starts in the slushpile. Most writers never get out of it. They simply get tired of receiving rejections and eventually quit writing.

At both *Analog* and *Omni* I personally read all the incoming manuscripts. There were no first readers, no assistant readers. The editor read everything. It made for some very long days. And nights. Long—and frustrating. Because in story after story I saw the same basic mistakes being made, the same fundamentals of storytelling being ignored. Stories that began with good ideas or that had stretches of good writing in them would fall apart and become unpublishable simply because the writer had over-looked—or never knew—the basic principles of storytelling.

There are good ways and poor ways to build a story, just as there are good ways and poor ways to build a house. If the writer does not use good techniques, the story will collapse, just as when a builder uses poor techniques his building collapses.

Every writer must bring three major factors to each story that he writes. They are ideas, artistry and craftsmanship.

Ideas will be discussed later in this book; suffice it to say for now that they are nowhere as difficult to find and develop as most new writers fear.

Artistry depends on the individual writer's talent and commitment to writing. No one can teach artistry to a writer, although many have tried. Artistry depends almost entirely on what is inside the writer: innate talent, heart, guts and drive.

Craftsmanship can be taught, and it is the one area where new writers consistently fall short. In most cases it is simple lack of craftsmanship that prevents a writer from leaving the slushpile. Like a carpenter who has never learned to drive nails straight, writers who have not learned craftsmanship will get nothing but pain for their efforts. That is why I have written this book: to help new writers learn a few things about the craftsmanship that goes into successful stories.

THE PLAN OF THIS BOOK

The plan of this book is straightforward. I assume that you want to write publishable fiction, either short stories or novels. I will speak directly to you, just as if we were sitting together in my home discussing craftsmanship face to face.

First, we will talk about science fiction, its special requirements, its special satisfactions. The science fiction field is demanding, but it is the best place for new writers to begin their careers. It is vital, exciting, and offers a close and immediate interaction between readers and writers.

In the next section of the book we will talk about the four main aspects of fiction writing: character, background, conflict and plot. Four short stories of mine will serve as models to illustrate the points we discuss. There are myriads of better and more popular stories to use as examples, of course. I use four of my own because I know exactly how and why they came to be written, what problems they presented to the writer, when they were published, where they met my expectations, and where they failed.

Each of these four areas of study—character, background, conflict and plot—is divided into three parts. The section begins with the chapter "Character: Theory." After it, is the short story that serves as an example, followed by the chapter "Character: Practice," showing how the theoretical ideas were handled in the actual story. Then come chapters on background, conflict and plot: theory first, then a short story, followed by a chapter on practice using the story as an illustration.

Next will come a section specifically about writing novels. We will discuss the different demands that novels make on the writer and how successful novelists have met these challenges. We will deal with the things you need to do before you write a novel, and then the actual writing task. The next chapter, on marketing, will discuss how to go about selling your work, both novels and short fiction.

Finally, there will be a wrap-up section in which we discuss ideas, style, and a few other things.

WHAT THIS BOOK IS NOT

This book is not an exhaustive text on the techniques of writing. I assume that you know how to construct an English sentence and how to put sentences together into readable paragraphs. We will not spend a chapter, or even a few pages, discussing the importance of using strong verbs or the active versus the passive voice or the proper use of adjectives and adverbs. All these things you should have acquired in high school English classes. If you don't understand them now, go back and learn them before going any further.

There are many graduates of high school and college courses in creative writing who have been taught how to write lovely paragraphs, but who have never learned how to construct a story. Creative writing courses hardly ever teach story construction. This book deals with construction techniques. It is intended as a practical guide for those who want to write commercial fiction and sell it to magazine and book editors.

We will concentrate on the craft of writing, on the techniques of telling a story in print. Some critics may consider this too simple, too mechanistic, for aspiring writers to care about. But, as I said earlier, it is the poor craftsmanship of most stories that prevents them from being published.

Good story-writing certainly has a mechanical side to it. You cannot get readers interested in a wandering, pointless tale any more than you can get someone to buy a house that has no roof.

Since the time when storytelling began, probably back in the Ice Ages, people have developed workable, usable, successful techniques for telling their tales. Storytellers use those techniques today, whether they are sitting around a campfire or in a Hollywood office. The techniques have changed very little over the centuries because the human brain has not changed. We still receive information and assimilate it in our minds in the same way our ancestors did. Our basic neural wiring has not changed, so the techniques of storytelling, of putting information into that human neural wiring, are basically unchanged.

Homer used these techniques. So did Goethe and Shakespeare.

And so will you, if and when you become a successful storyteller. I hope this book will help you along that path.

Chapter Two

Science Fiction

If science fiction is escapist, it's escape into reality.
  —*Isaac Asimov*

This book is basically about science fiction writing, although the techniques for writing science fiction can be used for any kind of fiction writing.

There are three main reasons for concentrating on science fiction, but before I enumerate them I should define exactly what I mean by *science fiction*.

DEFINITION

Science fiction stories are those in which some aspect of future science or high technology is so integral to the story that, if you take away the science or technology, the story collapses.

Think of *Frankenstein*. Take the scientific element out of Mary Wollstonecraft Shelley's novel and what is left? A failed medical student and not much more.

You may be surprised to realize that most of the books and magazine stories published under the science fiction rubric fail to meet this criterion. The science fiction category is very broad: it includes fantasy, horror, and speculative tales of the future in which science plays little or no part at all.

From here on, when I say science fiction, I mean stories that meet the definition given above. Other areas of the field I will call SF. The term *sci-fi*, which most science fiction writers loathe, I will reserve for those motion pictures that claim to be science fiction but are actually based on comic strips. Or worse.

THREE REASONS

The three reasons this book concentrates on science fiction story-writing are:

1. In today's commercial fiction market, SF is one of the few areas open to new writers, whether they are writing short stories or novels. Mysteries, gothics, romances, and other categories of commercial fiction are much more limited and specialized, especially for the short-story writer, but SF is as wide open as the infinite heavens. SF magazines actively seek new writers, and SF books consistently account for roughly 10 percent of the fiction books published each year in the United States. The SF community is quick to recognize new talent.

2. Science fiction presents to a writer challenges and problems that cannot be found in other forms of fiction. In addition to all the usual problems of writing, science fiction stories must also have strong and believable scientific or technical backgrounds. Isaac Asimov often declared that writing science fiction was more difficult than any other kind of writing. He should have known; he wrote everything from mysteries to learned tomes on the Bible and Shakespeare. If you can handle science fiction skillfully, chances are you will be able to write other types of fiction or nonfiction with ease.

3. Science fiction is the field in which I have done most of my work, both as a writer and an editor. Although most of my novels are written for the general audience, since they almost always deal with scientists and high technology they are usually marketed under the SF category. My eleven years as a magazine editor at *Analog* and *Omni* were strictly within the science fiction field, and I won six Science Fiction Achievement Awards (called the Hugo) for Best Professional Editor during that time.

THE LITERATURE OF IDEAS

Science fiction has become known as "the literature of ideas," so much so that some critics have disparagingly pointed out that many SF stories have The Idea as their hero, with very little else to recommend them. Ideas are important in science fiction. They are a necessary ingredient of any good SF tale. But the ideas themselves should not be the be-all and end-all of every story. (Ideas and idea-generation are discussed in chapter nineteen.)

Very often it is the idea content of good science fiction that attracts new writers to this exciting yet demanding field. (And please note that new writers are not necessarily youngsters; many men and women turn to writing fiction after establishing successful careers in other fields.) Science fiction's sense of wonder attracts new writers. And why not? Look at the playground they have for themselves! There's the entire universe of stars and galaxies, and all of the past, present, and future to write about. Science fiction stories can be set anywhere and anytime. There's interstellar flight, time travel, immortality, genetic engineering, nanotechnology, behavior control, telepathy and other types of extrasensory perception (ESP), colonies in space, new technologies, explorations of the vast cosmos or the inner landscapes of the mind.

John W. Campbell, most influential of all science fiction editors, fondly compared science fiction to other forms of literature in this way: He would spread his arms wide (and he had long arms) and declaim, "This is science fiction! All the universe, past, present and future." Then he would hold up a thumb and forefinger about half an inch apart and say, "This is all the other kinds of fiction."

All the other kinds of fiction restrict themselves to the here-and-now, or to the known past. All other forms of fiction are set here on Earth, under a sky that is blue and ground that is solid beneath your feet. Science fiction deals with all of creation, of which our Earth and our time are merely a small part. Science fiction can vault far into the future or deep into the past.

But even more fascinating for the writer (and the reader) of science fiction is the way these ideas can be used to develop stories about people. That is what fiction is about—people. In science fiction, some of the "people" may not look very human; they may be alien creatures or intelligent robots or sentient sequoia trees. They may live on strange, wild, exotic worlds. Yet they will always face incredible problems and strive to surmount them. Sometimes they will win, sometimes lose. But they will always strive, because at the core of every good science fiction story is the very fundamental faith that we can use our own intelligence to understand the universe and solve our problems.

All those weird backgrounds and fantastic ideas, all those special ingredients of science fiction, are a set of tricks that writers use to place their characters in the desperate situations where they will have to do their very best, or their very worst, to survive. For fiction is an examination of the human spirit, placing that spirit in a crucible where we can test its true worth. In science fiction we can go far beyond the boundaries of the here-and-now to put that crucible any place and any time we want to, and make the testing fire as hot as can be imagined.

That is science fiction's special advantage and its special challenge: going beyond the boundaries of the here-and-now to test the human spirit in new and ever-more-powerful ways.

This means that the SF field can encompass a tremendous variety of story types, from the hard-core science-based fiction that I usually write to the softer SF of writers such as Ray Bradbury and Harlan Ellison, and from glitzy Hollywood "sci-fi" flicks to the various kinds of fantasy and horror that now crowd the SF field. Hard-core science fiction, the type that is based on the world as we know it, has been my life. I have been reading it since junior high school, writing it for more than four decades.

The Demand for Science Fiction

Over the past few years, several editors have told me that they are longing to see hard-core science fiction stories. They tell me they are glutted with soft SF and fantasy and other types of stories. There is a demand for science fiction material that is not being met by the writers.

Why is this so? Perhaps it is because honest science fiction is the toughest kind of fiction to write. Every time I hear the term "hard science fiction," I think to myself, "Hard? It's goddamned exhausting, that's what it is!"

Science Fiction's Special Requirements

Every good science fiction story must present to the reader a world that no one has ever seen before. You cannot take it for granted that the sky is blue, that chairs have legs, or that what goes up must come down. In a good science fiction story the writer is presenting a new world in a fresh universe. In addition to all the other things that a good story must accomplish, a good science fiction tale must present the ground rules—and use them consistently—without stopping the flow of the narrative.

In other forms of fiction the writer must create believable characters and set them in conflict to generate an interesting story. In science fiction the writer must do all this and much more. Where in the universe is the story set? Is it even in our universe? Are we in the future or the distant past? Is there a planet under our feet or are we dangling in zero gravity? The science fiction writer must set the stage carefully and show it to the reader without letting the stage settings steal the attention from the characters and their problems.

Indeed, one of the faults found with science fiction by outsiders is that all too frequently the underlying idea or the exotic background is all that the story has going for it. The characters, the plot, everything else becomes quite secondary to the ideas.

Where anything is possible, everything has to be explained. Yet the modern writer does not have the luxury of spending a chapter or two giving the life history of each major character, the way Victorian writers did. Or page after page of pseudoscientific justification for each new scientific wonder, the way the pulp magazines of the 1920s and 1930s did.

Very well then, if science fiction is so tough to write, why bother?

Because of its *power*, that's why.

Science Fiction's Special Satisfactions

This tremendous latitude, this ability to set a story anywhere and anytime, not only presents the writer with a massive set of problems, it also gives the writer the marvelous opportunity — and perhaps the responsibility — to offer a powerful commentary on the world of today by showing it reflected in an imaginary world of tomorrow (or, in some cases, of distant yesterdays).

Some people have praised science fiction for its predictions. Nuclear power, space flight, computers, and most of the technological trappings of today's world were predicted in science fiction tales more than half a century ago. More important, I think, is that science fiction stories also predicted the Cold War, the global population explosion, environmental pollution, and many of the social problems we are wrestling with today.

Picture the history of the human race as a vast migration through time, thousands of millions of people wandering through the centuries. The writers of science fiction are the scouts, the explorers, the pathfinders who venture out ahead and look over the landscape, then send back stories that warn of the harsh desert up ahead, the thorny paths to be avoided, or tales that dazzle us with reports of beautiful wooded hills and clear streams and sunny grasslands that lie just over the horizon.

Those who read science fiction never fall victim to future shock. They have seen the future in the stories we have written for them. That is a glittering aspiration for a writer. And a heavy responsibility.

Chapter Three

Character in Science Fiction
Character: Theory

What is either a picture or a novel that is not character?
     —Henry James

All fiction is based on character.
That is, every fiction story hinges on the writer's handling of the people in the story. In particular, it is the central character, or protagonist, who makes the difference between a good story and a bad one.

In fact, you can define a story as the prose description of a character attempting to solve a problem—nothing more. And nothing less.

In science fiction, the character need not be a human being. Science fiction stories have been written in which the protagonist is a robot, an alien from another world, a supernatural being, an animal or even a plant. But in each case, the story was successful only if the protagonist—no matter what he/she/it looked like or was made of—behaved like a human being.

Readers come to stories for enjoyment. They do not want to be bored or confused. They do not want to be preached to. If a reader starts a story about a machine or a tree or a pintail duck, and the protagonist has no human traits at all—it simply grinds its gears or sways in the wind or lays eggs—the reader will quickly put the story down and turn to something else. But give the protagonist a human problem, such as survival, and let it struggle to solve that problem, and the reader will be able to enjoy the story.

A story is like any other form of entertainment: It must catch the audience's interest and then hold it. A printed story has enormous advantages over every other form of entertainment, because the written word can appeal directly to the reader's imagination. A writer can unlock the reader's imagination and take the reader on an exciting journey to strange and wonderful lands, using nothing more than ink and paper. A writer does not need a crew of actors, directors, musicians, stagehands, cameramen or props, sets, curtains, lights. All a writer needs is a writing tool with which to speak directly to the reader.

On the other hand, the writer never meets the reader. You can't stand at a reader's elbow and explain the things that puzzle him; you can't advise the reader to skip the next few paragraphs because they are really not necessary to understand the story and should have been taken out. The writer must put down everything she wants to say, in print, and hope that the reader will see and hear and feel and taste and smell the things that the writer wants to get across. You are asking the reader to understand what was in your mind while you were writing, to understand it by deciphering those strange ink marks on the paper.

Your job as a writer is to make the reader live in your story. You must make the reader forget that he is sitting in a rather uncomfortable chair, squinting at the page in poor light, while all sorts of distractions poke at him. You want your reader to believe that he is actually in the world of your imagination, the world you have created, climbing up that mountain you've written about, struggling against the cold and ice to find the treasure that you planted up at the peak.

The easiest way—in fact, the only good way—to make the reader live in your story is to give the reader a character that he wants to be.

Let the reader imagine that she is Anna Karenina, facing a tragic choice between love and family. Or David Hawkins being chased by pirates across Treasure Island. Let the reader live the life of Nick Adams or Tugboat Annie or Sherlock Holmes or Cinderella.

MAKING CHARACTERS LIVE

How do you do this? There are two major things to keep in mind.

First, remember that every story is essentially the description of a character struggling to solve a problem. Pick your central character with care. The protagonist must be interesting enough, and have a grievous-enough problem, to make the reader care about her. Often the protagonist is called the viewpoint character, because the story is told from that character's point of view. It is the protagonist's story that you are telling, and she must be strong enough to carry the story.

Select a protagonist (or viewpoint character) who has great strengths and at least one glaring weakness, and then give him a staggering problem. Think of Hamlet, Shakespeare's Prince of Denmark. He was strong, intelligent, handsome, loyal, a natural leader; yet he was indecisive, uncertain of himself, and this was his eventual undoing. If Hamlet had been asked to lead an army or woo a lady or get straight As at the university, he could have done it easily. But Shakespeare gave him a problem that preyed on his weakness, not his strength. This is what every good writer must do. Once you have decided who your protagonist will be and you know his strengths and weaknesses, hit him where it hurts most! Develop an instinct for the jugular. Give your main character a problem that she cannot solve, and then make it as difficult as possible for her to struggle out of her dilemma.

I want to borrow a marvelous technique from William Foster-Harris, who was a fine teacher of writing at the University of Oklahoma. He hit upon the technique of visualizing story characters' problems in the form of a simple equation: *Emotion A* vs. *Emotion B*. For example, you might depict Hamlet as a case of *revenge* vs. *self-doubt*. Think of the characters you have loved best in the stories you have read. Each of them was torn by conflicting emotions, from the Biblical patriarch Abraham's *obedience* vs. *love*, when commanded by God to sacrifice his son Isaac, to the *greed* vs. *loyalty* often displayed by my own quixotic character, Sam Gunn.

Whenever you start to think about a character for a story, even a secondary character, try to sum up his or her essential characteristics in this simple formula. Don't let the simplicity of this approach fool you. If you can't capture a character by a straightforward *emotion* vs. *emotion* equation, then you haven't thought out the character well enough to begin writing. Of course, for minor characters this isn't necessary. But it certainly is vital for the protagonist, and it can be just as important for the secondary characters, too.

With this approach, you begin to understand that the protagonist's real problem is inside her head. The basic conflict of the story, the mainspring that drives it onward, is an emotional conflict inside the mind of the protagonist. The other conflicts in the story stem from this source, as we will see in more detail in the chapters on conflict.

And never let the protagonist know that she will win! Many stories are written in which a very capable and interesting protagonist faces a monumental set of problems. Then she goes about solving them without ever trembling, doubting herself or even perspiring! The protagonist knows she is safe and will be successful, because the writer knows that the story will end happily. This makes for an unbelievable and boring story. Who is going to worry about the world cracking in half when the heroine doesn't worry about it? Certainly not the reader!

The reader must be hanging on tenterhooks of doubt and suspense up until the very end of the story. Which means that the protagonist must be equally in doubt about the outcome.

And there is always a price to be paid. In a well-crafted story the protagonist cannot win unless he surrenders something of inestimable value to himself. In other words, he has got to lose something, and the reader will be in a fever of anticipation trying to figure out what he is going to lose.

The unruffled, supercool, utterly capable hero is one of the most widespread stereotypes of poor fiction, and especially of poor SF. Like all stereotypes, he makes for a boring and unbelievable story.

When a writer stocks a story with stereotypes—the brilliant but naive scientist; the jut-jawed, two-fisted hero; the beautiful but helpless young woman; the evil, reptilian aliens—the writer is merely signaling to the editor that he hasn't thought very deeply about his story.

Stereotype characters are prefabricated parts. Somebody else created these types long ago, and the new writer is merely borrowing them. They are old, shopworn, and generally made of cardboard. A good writer is like a good architect: Every story he creates should be an original, with characters and settings designed specifically for that individual story. Not somebody else's prefabricated parts.

Writers who go into the prefab business are called hacks, and a new writer who starts as a hack never gets very far. It is bad enough to turn into a hack once you have become established; many popular writers on the best-seller lists have done that.

Look around you. You are surrounded by characters every day. How many stereotypes do you see? A jovial Irishman? A singing Italian? A lovesick teenager? A chalk-dusty school-teacher? An arrogant policeman? An officious administrator?

Look a little deeper. If you begin to study these people and get to know them, you will find that every one is an individual. Each has a unique personality, a distinct set of problems, habits, joys and fears. These are the characters you should write about. Watch them carefully. Study their strengths and weaknesses. Stress the points that make them different from everyone else, the traits that are uniquely theirs.

Ask yourself what kinds of problems would hurt them the worst. Then get to your keyboard and tell the world about it.

You might think that the people around you are hardly material for a science fiction story. Think again. People are people, and we will carry our human traits and problems to the farthest corners of the universe. Good science fiction stories, like all good fiction, are about people.

HANDLING POINT OF VIEW

In a short story, it is important to show the entire story through the protagonist's point of view. Viewpoint can shift from one character to another in a novel, if it is absolutely necessary, but within the brief confines of a short story it is best to stick to one viewpoint character and show the entire tale through that character's eyes.

Even if you write the story in the third person, put nothing on paper that the protagonist has not experienced firsthand. In a novel, where you may shift viewpoint from one character to another, it is best to write each individual scene from one character's viewpoint alone. In a short story, I repeat, tell the entire story from the protagonist's point of view.

This limits you, I know. The protagonist must be in every scene, and you can't tell the reader anything that the protagonist does not know. But in return for these problems you get a story that is immediate and real. When the protagonist is puzzled, the reader is puzzled; when the protagonist feels pain, the reader aches; when the protagonist wins against all odds, the reader triumphs. In other words, the reader has been living the story, not merely reading some words off a page.

You might be tempted to write the story in the first person:

> I felt the wind whipping at my clothes, cold and sharp and stinging. My pulse was roaring in my ears. I looked down; it was a long way to fall. . . .

But you can get almost the same sense of immediacy from a third-person viewpoint, if you restrict yourself to writing only what the protagonist senses:

> He felt the wind whipping at his clothes, cold and sharp and stinging. His pulse was roaring in his ears. He looked down; it was a long way to fall. . . .

This kind of close and immediate third-person viewpoint has the benefit of being far enough removed from the protagonist so that you can be a little more objective about him. For example, it is very tough to make your protagonist describe himself:

> I'm six feet tall and very solidly built. My hair is blond and wavy; women like to run their fingers through it.

In the third-person viewpoint, the same description does not sound obnoxious at all:

> Jack was six feet tall and very solidly built. His hair was blond and wavy; women liked to run their fingers through it.

Also, when you write in the third person, you can step away from the protagonist if it is absolutely necessary to tell the reader something that the protagonist does not know:

> Despite Jack's good looks, Sheryl hated him. She had never let him know this; she wanted him to think. . . .

This kind of information sometimes has to be given to the reader. But think long and hard before you step away from your viewpoint character. It can be a very dangerous step, more confusing to the reader than helpful. The best rule is to stay with the protagonist at all times, unless it is absolutely impossible to say what needs to be said.

Sensory Reality

Use your protagonist's five senses to make certain that the story has as much sensory reality as possible. Check each page of your manuscript to see how many of the protagonist's senses are used. If a page has nothing but what the protagonist saw, or only what she heard, rewrite that page so that the sense of touch or taste or smell comes into play. It is astounding how much more vivid that makes the story.

Where do you find a strong protagonist, and what kind of problems can you give her?

Every story you write will be at least partially autobiographical, and every protagonist you create will contain more than a little of yourself. That is what makes writing such an emotional pursuit: You are revealing yourself, putting your heart and guts out on public display every time you write a story. When a story is rejected or a published story is battered by the critics or it fails to sell well, it is as if you yourself are being kicked, folded, stapled and mutilated. When a story sells or someone tells you she liked it or it wins an award, there is no amount of money in the world that can buy that feeling of elation. Each story you write is a part of you. Writers don't use ink, they use their own blood. And the reason most people stop writing is they can't stand the emotional strain, or they don't have the emotional need to write.

All this adds up to a simple fact: Your protagonists will be you, to a large degree, together with some mixture of people you know. Beginning writers are always advised to write about people and things that they know firsthand. Experienced writers are never told this, because they have learned the lesson thoroughly. No one ever writes about anything that she has not experienced firsthand. Never. It cannot be done.

Really? In a few moments you are going to read "Fifteen Miles," a story about a man trying to walk across fifteen miles of the moon's surface, an astronaut who is dragging back the injured body of a fellow astronaut. I have not been to the moon. I have never had to carry an injured friend through a wilderness for fifteen feet, let alone fifteen miles. So, where is my firsthand experience?

I know the people in that story firsthand. I have lived with Chester Arthur Kinsman in my head for almost half a century. I have written dozens of short stories and several novels about him. Almost all of them were rejected, and even "Fifteen Miles" was bounced by the first editor I sent it to. Kinsman and I learned to write together. Father Lemoyne and Bok, the astronomer, are also people I know, composites of many people I have met and worked with over the years.

"Fifteen Miles" was written before the Apollo program put astronauts on the moon. But it could not have been written before space probes such as *Ranger* and *Surveyor* photographed the lunar surface so thoroughly. I wrote the story literally surrounded by photos and maps of the area in which the action takes place. I worked in the aerospace industry for many years and became familiar with the kinds of equipment that will be used when we return to the moon for longer explorations. I have met and worked with the people involved in the space program. I have watched and read volumes of testimony before congressional committees, which is where the quotation that opens the story comes from.

All this is firsthand experience, of a kind. To this experience must come a touch of imagination. That touch came to me when I read Jack London's story "To Light a Fire." As I lived London's story and felt the bitter cold of the Yukon freezing me, somewhere deep in the back of my mind a tiny voice said to me, "If Jack London were alive today, he'd still be writing stories about men struggling against the wilderness . . . but they'd be set on the moon, rather than on Earth."

Immediately the title, "Fifteen Miles," formed itself in my mind. I wanted to do a story about how difficult it might be to walk across fifteen miles of lunar landscape.

But that was just the bare idea. There was no story in my head until good old Chet Kinsman popped up and said, "Hey, this is my story. Remember where you left me last time, in 'Test in Orbit'? 'Fifteen Miles' is the sequel to that story."

He was right. I gave Kinsman the task of making that fifteen-mile walk and burdened him with a set of problems to make the situation as difficult as possible. I nearly killed him.

Which is what good story-writing is all about.

A CHARACTER CHECKLIST

Listed on the following page are the seven major points I have made in this chapter. We will examine them again in chapter five to see how each point was followed in "Fifteen Miles."

1. In a good story the reader forgets where he is and lives in the story; the reader wants to *be* the protagonist.

2. The protagonist must be admirable, or at least likable, but he should have at least one glaring weakness that forms the underlying tension that drives the character's behavior. Capture those conflicting traits in a simple *emotion* vs. *emotion* equation.

3. The protagonist must struggle to solve his problems. That struggle is the backbone of the story.

4. Avoid stereotypes!

5. Study the people around you; draw your characters from life.

6. Show the story from the protagonist's point of view.

7. Use all five senses: Describe what your characters see, hear, touch, taste and smell.

Chapter Four

Character in Science Fiction

Fifteen Miles

A Complete Short Story

Sen. Anderson: Does that mean that man's mobility on the moon will be severely limited?

Mr. Webb: Yes, Sir; it is going to be severely limited, Mr. Chairman. The moon is a rather hostile place . . .
        —U.S. Senate Hearings on National Space Goals, 23 August 1965

Any word from him yet?"

"Huh? No, nothing."

Kinsman swore to himself as he stood on the open platform of the little lunar rocket jumper.

"Say, where are you now?" The astronomer's voice sounded gritty with static in Kinsman's helmet earphones.

"Up on the rim. He must've gone inside the damned crater."

"The rim? How'd you get—"

"Found a flat spot for the jumper. Don't think I walked this far, do you? I'm not as nutty as the priest."

"But you're supposed to stay down here on the plain! The crater's off limits."

"Tell it to our holy friar. He's the one who marched up here. I'm just following the seismic rigs he's been planting every three-four miles."

He could sense Bok shaking his head. "Kinsman, if there're twenty officially approved ways to do a job, you'll pick the twenty-second."

"If the first twenty-one are lousy."

"You're not going inside the crater, are you? It's too risky."

Kinsman almost laughed. "You think sitting in that aluminum casket of yours is *safe*?"

The earphones went silent. With a scowl, Kinsman wished for the tenth time in an hour that he could scratch his twelve-day beard. *Get zipped into the suit and the itches start.* He didn't need a mirror to know that his face was haggard, sleepless, and his black beard was mean looking.

He stepped down from the jumper—a rocket motor with a railed platform and some equipment on it, nothing more—and planted his boots on the solid rock of the ringwall's crest. With a twist of his shoulders to settle the weight of the pressure suit's bulky backpack, he shambled over to the packet of seismic instruments and fluorescent marker that the priest had left there.

"He came right up to the top, and now he's off on the yellow brick road, playing moon explorer. Stupid bastard."

Reluctantly, he looked into the crater Alphonsus. The brutally short horizon cut across its middle, but the central peak stuck its worn head up among the solemn stars. Beyond it was nothing but dizzying blackness, an abrupt end to the solid world and the beginning of infinity.

Damn the priest! God's gift to geology . . . and I've got to play guardian angel for him.

"Any sign of him?"

Kinsman turned back and looked outward from the crater. He could see the lighted radio mast and squat return rocket, far below on the plain. He even convinced himself that he saw the mound of rubble marking their buried base shelter, where Bok lay curled safely in his bunk. It was two days before sunrise, but the Earthlight lit the plain well enough.

"Sure," Kinsman answered. "He left me a big map with an X to mark the treasure."

"Don't get sore at me!"

"Why not? You're sitting inside. I've got to find our fearless geologist."

"Regulations say one man's got to be in the base at all times."

But not the same one man, Kinsman flashed silently.

"Anyway," Bok went on, "he's got a few hours' oxygen left. Let him putter around inside the crater for a while. He'll come back."

"Not before his air runs out. Besides, he's officially missing. Missed two check-in calls. I'm supposed to scout his last known position. Another of those sweet regs."

Silence again. Bok didn't like being alone in the base, Kinsman knew.

"Why don't you come on back," the astronomer's voice returned, "until he calls in. Then you can get him with the jumper. You'll be running out of air yourself before you can find him inside the crater."

"I'm supposed to try."

"But why? You sure don't think much of him. You've been tripping all over yourself trying to stay clear of him when he's inside the base."

Kinsman suddenly shuddered. *So it shows! If you're not careful, you'll tip them both off.*

Aloud he said, "I'm going to look around. Give me an hour. Better call Earthside and tell them what's going on. Stay in the shelter until I come back." *Or until the relief crew shows up.*

"You're wasting your time. And taking an unnecessary chance."

"Wish me luck," Kinsman answered.

"Good luck. I'll sit tight here."

Despite himself, Kinsman grinned. Shutting off the radio, he said to himself, "I know damned well you'll sit tight. Two scientific adventurers. One goes over the hill and the other stays in his bunk two weeks straight."

He gazed out at the bleak landscape, surrounded by starry emptiness. Something caught at his memory:

"They can't scare me with their empty spaces," he muttered. There was more to the verse but he couldn't recall it.

"Can't scare me," he repeated softly, shuffling to the inner rim. He walked very carefully and tried, from inside the cumbersome helmet, to see exactly where he was placing his feet.

The barren slopes fell away in gently terraced steps until, more than half a mile below, they melted into the crater floor. *Looks easy . . . too easy.* With a shrug that was weighted down by the pressure suit, Kinsman started to descend into the crater.

He picked his way across the gravelly terraces and crawled feet first down the breaks between them. The bare rocks were slippery and sometimes sharp. Kinsman went slowly, step by step, trying to make certain he didn't puncture the aluminized fabric of his suit.

His world was cut off now and circled by the dark rocks. The only sounds he knew were the creakings of the suit's joints, the electrical hum of its motor, the faint whir of the helmet's air blower, and his own heavy breathing. Alone, all alone. A solitary microcosm. One living creature in the one universe.

They cannot scare me with their empty spaces Between stars — on stars where no human race is.

There was still more to it: the tag line that he couldn't remember.

Finally he had to stop. The suit was heating up too much from his exertion. He took a marker beacon and planted it on the broken ground. The moon's soil, churned by meteors and whipped into a frozen froth, had an unfinished look about it, as though somebody had been blacktopping the place but stopped before he could apply the final smoothing touches.

From a pouch on his belt Kinsman took a small spool of wire. Plugging one end into the radio outlet on his helmet, he held the spool at arm's length and released the catch. He couldn't see it in the dim light, but he felt the spring fire the wire antenna a hundred yards or so upward and out into the crater.

"Father Lemoyne," he called as the antenna drifted in the moon's easy gravity. "Father Lemoyne, can you hear me? This is Kinsman."

No answer.

Okay. Down another flight.

After two more stops and nearly an hour of sweaty descent, Kinsman got his answer.

"Here . . . I'm here. . . ."

"Where?" Kinsman snapped. "Do something. Make a light."

". . . can't . . ." The voice faded out.

Kinsman reeled in the antenna and fired it out again. "Where the hell are you?"

A cough, with pain behind it. "Shouldn't have done it. Disobeyed. And no water, nothing . . ."

Great! Kinsman frowned. *He's either hysterical or delirious. Or both.*

After firing the spool antenna again, Kinsman flicked on the lamp atop his helmet and looked at the radio direction finder dial on his forearm. The priest had his suit radio open and the carrier beam was coming through even though he was not talking. The gauges alongside the radio finder reminded Kinsman that he was about halfway down on his oxygen, and more than an hour had elapsed since he had spoken to Bok.

"I'm trying to zero in on you," Kinsman said. "Are you hurt? Can you . . ."

"Don't, don't, don't. I disobeyed and now I've got to pay for it. Don't trap yourself, too . . ." The heavy, reproachful voice lapsed into a mumble that Kinsman couldn't understand.

Trapped. Kinsman could picture it. The priest was using a canister-suit: a one-man walking cabin, a big plexidomed rigid can with flexible arms and legs sticking out of it. You could live in it for days at a time but it was too clumsy for climbing. Which is why the crater was off limits.

He must've fallen and now he's stuck.

"The sin of pride," he heard the priest babbling. "God forgive us our pride. I wanted to find water; the greatest discovery a man can make on the moon. Pride, nothing but pride."

Kinsman walked slowly, shifting his eyes from the direction finder to the roiled, pocked ground underfoot. He jumped across an eight-foot drop between terraces. The finder's needle snapped to zero.

"Your radio still on?"

"No use . . . go back . . ."

The needle stayed fixed. *Either I busted it or I'm right on top of him.*

He turned full circle, scanning the rough ground as far as his light could reach. No sign of the canister. Kinsman stepped to the terrace edge. Kneeling with deliberate care, so that his backpack wouldn't unbalance and send him sprawling down the tumbled rocks, he peered over.

In a zigzag fissure a few yards below him was the priest, a giant armored insect gleaming white in the glare of the lamp, feebly waving its one free arm.

"Can you get up?" Kinsman saw that all the weight of the cumbersome suit was on the pinned arm. *Banged up his back-pack, too.*

The priest was mumbling again. It sounded like Latin.

"Can you get up?" Kinsman repeated.

"Trying to find the secrets of natural creation . . . storming heaven with rockets. . . . We say we're seeking knowledge, but we're really after our own glory . . ."

Kinsman frowned. He couldn't see the older man's face behind the canister's heavily tinted window.

"I'll have to get the jumper."

The priest rambled on, coughing spasmodically. Kinsman started back across the terrace.

"Pride leads to death," he heard in his earphones. "You know that, Kinsman. It's pride that makes us murderers."

The shock boggled Kinsman's knees. He turned, trembling. "What . . . did you say?"

"It's hidden. The water is here, hidden. Frozen in fissures. Strike the rock and bring forth water . . . like Moses. Not even God Himself was going to hide this secret from me . . ."

"What did you say," Kinsman whispered, completely cold inside, "about murder?"

"I know you, Kinsman . . . anger and pride . . . Destroy not my soul with men of blood . . . whose right hands are . . . are . . ."

Kinsman ran away. He fought back toward the crater rim, storming the terraces blindly, scrabbling up the inclines with four-yard-high jumps. Twice he had to turn up the air blower in his helmet to clear the sweaty fog from his faceplate. He didn't dare stop. He raced on, his heart pounding until he could hear nothing else.

But in his mind he still saw those savage few minutes in orbit, when he had been with the Air Force, when he became a killer. He had won a medal for that secret mission; a medal and a conscience that never slept.

Finally he reached the crest. Collapsing on the deck of the jumper, he forced himself to breathe normally again, forced himself to sound normal as he called Bok.

The astronomer said guardedly, "It sounds as though he's dying."

"I think his regenerator's shot. His air must be pretty foul by now."

"No sense going back for him, I guess."

Kinsman hesitated. "Maybe I can get the jumper down close to him." *He found out about me.*

"You'll never get him back in time. And you're not supposed

to take the jumper near the crater, let alone inside of it. It's too dangerous."

"You want me to just let him die?" *He's hysterical. If he babbles about me where Bok can hear it . . .*

"Listen," the astronomer said, his voice rising, "you can't leave me stuck here with both of you gone! I know the regulations, Kinsman. You're not allowed to risk yourself or the third man on the team to help a man in trouble."

"I know. I know." *But it wouldn't look right for me to start minding regulations now. Even Bok doesn't expect me to.*

"You don't have enough oxygen in your suit to get down there and back again," Bok insisted.

"I can tap some from the jumper's propellant tank."

"But that's crazy! You'll get yourself stranded!"

"Maybe." *It's an Air Force secret. No discharge; just transferred to the space agency. If they find out about it now, I'll be finished. Everybody'll know. No place to hide . . . newspapers, TV, everybody!*

"You're going to kill yourself over that priest. And you'll be killing me, too!"

"He's probably dead by now," Kinsman said. "I'll just put a marker beacon there, so another crew can get him when the time comes. I won't be long."

"But the regulations . . ."

"They were written Earthside. The brass never planned on something like this. I've got to go back, just to make sure."

He flew the jumper back down the crater's inner slope, leaning over the platform railing to see his marker beacons as well as listening to their tinny radio beeping. In a few minutes, he was easing the spraddle-legged platform down on the last terrace before the helpless priest.

"Father Lemoyne."

Kinsman stepped off the jumper and made it to the edge of the fissure in four lunar strides. The white shell was inert, the free arm unmoving.

"Father Lemoyne!"

Kinsman held his breath and listened. Nothing . . . wait . . . the faintest, faintest breathing. More like gasping. Quick, shallow, desperate.

"You're dead," Kinsman heard himself mutter. "Give it up,

you're finished. Even if I got you out of here, you'd be dead before I could get you back to the base."

The priest's faceplate was opaque to him; he only saw the reflected spot of his own helmet lamp. But his mind filled with the shocked face he once saw in another visor, a face that just realized it was dead.

He looked away, out to the too-close horizon and the uncompromising stars beyond. Then he remembered the rest of it:

> They cannot scare me with their empty spaces
> Between stars — on stars where no human race is.
> I have it in me so much nearer home
> To scare myself with my own desert places.

Like an automaton, Kinsman turned back to the jumper. His mind was blank now. Without thought, without even feeling, he rigged a line from the jumper's tiny winch to the metal lugs in the canister-suit's chest. Then he took apart the platform railing and wedged three rejoined sections into the fissure above the fallen man, to form a hoisting angle. Looping the line over the projecting arm, he started the winch.

He climbed down into the fissure and set himself as solidly as he could on the bare, scoured smooth rock. Grabbing the priest's armored shoulders, he guided the oversized canister up from the crevice, while the winch strained silently.

The railing arm gave way when the priest was only partway up, and Kinsman felt the full weight of the monstrous suit crush down on him. He sank to his knees, gritting his teeth to keep from crying out. Then the winch took up the slack. Grunting, fumbling, pushing, he scrabbled up the rocky slope with his arms wrapped halfway round the big canister's middle. He let the winch drag them to the jumper's edge, then reached out and shut off the motor.

With only a hard breath's pause, Kinsman snapped down the suit's supporting legs, so the priest could stay upright even though unconscious. Then he clambered onto the platform and took the oxygen line from the rocket tankage. Kneeling at the bulbous suit's shoulders, he plugged the line into its emergency air tank.

The older man coughed once. That was all.

Kinsman leaned back on his heels. His faceplate was fogging

over again. Or was it fatigue blurring his vision?

The regenerator was hopelessly smashed, he saw. *The old bird must've been breathing his own juices.* When the emergency tank registered full, he disconnected the oxygen line and plugged it into a fitting below the regenerator.

"If you're dead, this is probably going to kill me, too," Kinsman said. He purged the entire suit, forcing the contaminating fumes out and replacing them with the oxygen that the jumper's rocket needed to get them back to the base.

He was close enough now to see through the canister's tinted visor. The priest's face was grizzled, eyes closed. Its usual smile was gone; the mouth hung open limply.

Kinsman hauled him up onto the rail-less platform and strapped him down on the deck. Then he went to the controls and inched the throttle forward just enough to give them the barest minimum of lift.

The jumper almost made it to the crest before its rocket died and bumped them gently on one of the terraces. There was a small emergency tank of oxygen that could have carried them a little farther, Kinsman knew. But he and the priest would need it for breathing.

"Wonder how many Jesuits have been carried home on their shields?" he asked himself as he unbolted the section of decking that the priest was lying on. By threading the winch line through the bolt holes, he made a sort of sled, which he carefully lowered to the ground. Then he took down the emergency oxygen tank and strapped it to the deck-section, too.

Kinsman wrapped the line around his fists and leaned against the burden. Even in the moon's light gravity, it was like trying to haul a truck.

"Down to less than one horsepower," he grunted, straining forward.

For once he was glad that the scoured rocks had been smoothed clean by micrometeors. He would climb a few steps, wedge himself as firmly as he could, and drag the sled up to him. It took a painful half-hour to reach the ringwall crest.

He could see the base again, tiny and remote as a dream. "All downhill from here," he mumbled.

He thought he heard a groan.

"That's it," he said, pushing the sled over the crest, down the gentle outward slope. "That's it. Stay with it. Don't you die on me. Don't put me through this for nothing!"

"Kinsman!" Bok's voice. "Are you all right?"

The sled skidded against a yard-high rock. Scrambling after it, Kinsman answered, "I'm bringing him in. Just shut up and leave us alone. I think he's alive. Now stop wasting my breath."

Pull it free. Push to get it started downhill again. Strain to hold it back . . . don't let it get away from you. Haul it out of craterlets. Watch your step, don't fall.

"Too damned much uphill in this downhill."

Once he sprawled flat and knocked his helmet against the edge of the improvised sled. He must have blacked out for a moment. Weakly, he dragged himself up to the oxygen tank and refilled his suit's supply. Then he checked the priest's suit and topped off his tank.

"Can't do that again," he said to the silent priest. "Don't know if we'll make it. Maybe we can. If neither one of us has sprung a leak. Maybe . . ."

Time slid away from him. The past and future dissolved into an endless now, a forever of pain and struggle, with the heat of his toil welling up in Kinsman drenchingly.

"Why don't you say something?" Kinsman panted at the priest. "You can't die. Understand me? You can't die! I've got to explain it to you . . . I didn't mean to kill her. I didn't even know she was a girl. You can't tell, can't even see a face until you're too close. She must've been just as scared as I was. She tried to kill me. I was inspecting their satellite . . . how'd I know their cosmonaut was a scared kid? I could've pushed her off, didn't have to kill her. But the first thing I knew I was ripping her air lines open. I didn't know she was a girl, not until it was too late. It doesn't make any difference, but I didn't know it, I didn't know . . ."

They reached the foot of the ringwall and Kinsman dropped to his knees. "Couple more miles now . . . straight-away . . . only a couple more . . . miles." His vision was blurred, and something in his head was buzzing angrily.

Staggering to his feet, he lifted the line over his shoulder and slogged ahead. He could just make out the lighted tip of the base's radio mast.

"Leave him, Chet," Bok's voice pleaded from somewhere. "You can't make it unless you leave him!"

"Shut . . . up."

One step after another. Don't think, don't count. Blank your mind. Be a mindless plow horse. Plod along, one step at a time. Steer for the radio mast. Just a few . . . more miles.

"Don't die on me. Don't you . . . die on me. You're my ticket back. Don't die on me, priest . . . don't die . . ."

It all went dark. First in spots, then totally. Kinsman caught a glimpse of the barren landscape tilting weirdly, then the grave stars slid across his view, then darkness.

"I tried," he heard himself say in a far, far distant voice. "I tried."

For a moment or two he felt himself falling, dropping effortlessly into blackness. Then even that sensation died and he felt nothing at all.

A faint vibration buzzed at him. The darkness began to shift, turn gray at the edges. Kinsman opened his eyes and saw the low, curved ceiling of the underground base. The noise was the electrical machinery that lit and warmed and brought good air to the tight little shelter.

"You okay?" Bok leaned over him. His chubby face was frowning worriedly.

Kinsman weakly nodded.

"Father Lemoyne's going to pull through," Bok said, stepping out of the cramped space between the two bunks. The priest was awake but unmoving, his eyes staring blankly upward. His canister-suit had been removed and one arm was covered with a plastic cast.

Bok explained. "I've been getting instructions from the Earth-side medics. They're sending a team up; should be here in another thirty hours. He's in shock, and his arm's broken. Otherwise he seems pretty good . . . exhausted, but no permanent damage."

Kinsman pulled himself up to a sitting position on the bunk and leaned his back against the curving metal wall. His helmet and boots were off, but he was still wearing the rest of his pressure suit.

"You went out and got us," he realized.

Bok nodded. "You were only about a mile away. I could hear you on the radio. Then you stopped talking. I had to go out."

"You saved my life."

"And you saved the priest's."

Kinsman stopped a moment, remembering. "I did a lot of raving out there, didn't I?"

"Well . . . yes."

"Any of it intelligible?"

Bok wormed his shoulders uncomfortably. "Sort of. It's, uh . . . it's all on the automatic recorder, you know. All conversations. Nothing I can do about it."

That's it. Now everybody knows.

"You haven't heard the best of it, though," Bok said. He went to the shelf at the end of the priest's bunk and took a little plastic container. "Look at this."

Kinsman took the container. Inside was a tiny fragment of ice, half melted into water.

"It was stuck in the cleats of his boots. It's really water! Tests out okay, and I even snuck a taste of it. It's water all right."

"He found it after all," Kinsman said. "He'll get into the history books now." *And he'll have to watch his pride even more.*

Bok sat on the shelter's only chair. "Chet, about what you were saying out there . . ."

Kinsman expected tension, but instead he felt only numb. "I know. They'll hear the tapes Earthside."

"There've been rumors about an Air Force guy killing a cosmonaut during a military mission, but I never thought—I mean. . . ."

"The priest figured it out," Kinsman said. "Or at least he guessed it."

"It must've been rough on you," Bok said.

"Not as rough as what happened to her."

"What'll they do about you?"

Kinsman shrugged. "I don't know. It might get out to the press. Probably I'll be grounded. Unstable. It could be nasty."

"I'm . . . sorry." Bok's voice tailed off helplessly.

"It doesn't matter."

Surprised, Kinsman realized that he meant it. He sat straight upright. "It doesn't matter anymore. They can do whatever they want to. I can handle it. Even if they ground me and throw me to the newsmen . . . I think I can take it. I did it, and it's over with, and I can take what I have to take."

Father Lemoyne's free arm moved slightly. "It's all right," he whispered hoarsely. "It's all right."

The priest turned his face toward Kinsman. His gaze moved from the astronaut's eyes to the plastic container, still in Kinsman's hands, and back again.

"It's all right," he repeated. "It wasn't hell we were in; it was purgatory. We'll come out all right." He smiled. Then he closed his eyes and his face relaxed into sleep. But the smile remained, strangely gentle in that bearded, haggard face; ready to meet the world or eternity.

Chapter Five

Character in Science Fiction

Character: Practice

Give him a compulsion and turn him loose!
   — Ray Bradbury

F ifteen Miles" dealt with three characters, and each of them had a problem. Chet Kinsman was the viewpoint character, of course — the protagonist. Everything in the story was seen from his point of view. Without him and his problems, there would have been no story.

Notice that Kinsman had problems, plural. That is one major difference between the protagonist of a story and the other characters. Secondary characters can have one fundamental problem to solve. Minor characters need not have any problems at all. But the protagonist, the person whom the story is all about, the person whom the reader wants to be — the protagonist has a whole complex of problems.

All of Kinsman's problems stem from his fundamental emotional conflict of *guilt* vs. *duty*. Father Lemoyne is torn by *pride* vs. *obedience*. And Bok's problem is *fear* vs. *responsibility*.

Kinsman was raised in a Quaker family; he was not a terribly religious person, but his upbringing was in the pacifistic Quaker environment. Years before this story took place, he killed a Russian cosmonaut in hand-to-hand struggle during an orbital mission. It was a military mission, and both Kinsman and the Russian were military officers. (These stories were written in the 1960s, during the darkest days of the US-USSR Cold War. That is not to say, however, that someday the interests of the United States and Russia [or some other space-faring nation] might not again come into conflict.)

Usually, when military personnel battle and kill each other, it is not regarded as murder. But the cosmonaut was a woman, a fact that Kinsman did not know until he had pulled the airhose out of her helmet, suffocating her. His Quaker conscience has been screaming at him ever since, not just because he killed a fellow human being—in a situation where he might have gotten away without killing—but because it was a woman that he killed. Men can often justify murdering another man, but they have been raised to think of women as physically weaker than men. Men do not fight against women, as a rule. Even in the U.S. armed services, women's role in combat is severely curtailed. To kill a woman, to *murder* a woman in a hand-to-hand fight, is shocking to a man like Kinsman.

With that heavy conscience, Kinsman is locked into a two-week-long mission on the moon's surface with two other men. One of them is a priest, a symbol of conscience, a constant reminder to Kinsman that he is guilty of the sin of murder. So, even before the story actually begins, we have a very uncomfortable situation for our protagonist.

To this inner, mental problem we add an exterior, physical problem. More than one, in fact. The priest is lost, somewhere in the forbidden interior of the huge lunar crater (or ringwall) Alphonsus. The third member of the team, the astronomer Bok, is frightened to move out of the safety of their underground shelter.

This leaves Kinsman with a nasty set of problems. Where is Father Lemoyne? Is he hurt, and does he need help? Should Kinsman obey official regulations and leave the priest to his fate, or should he break the rules and try to find him?

CHAINS OF PROBLEMS AND PROMISES

The solution to one question, you notice, leads to the next question. This forms an interlocking chain of problems. The novelist Manuel Komroff chose another name for this: He called it an interlocking chain of promises, because each problem or question that you put before the reader implicitly promises a solution, an answer, something intriguing and exciting to lure the reader onward. Like a Western sheriff following an outlaw's trail, the reader will hunt from one problem to the next, eager to find each answer.

So you keep offering problems, asking questions, all through the story. And you never answer any question until you have raised at least one or two more, to be answered a few pages farther on. This keeps the reader turning pages anxiously, breathless to find out what happens next.

Once Kinsman finds Father Lemoyne, more problems confront him. Is the priest so near death that it would be pointless to try to rescue him? Would a rescue attempt work? Would it kill Kinsman himself? And then comes the most shocking problem of all: Father Lemoyne apparently knows about Kinsman's guilty secret. If Kinsman saves him, the priest may well reveal his secret to everyone. Kinsman will be disgraced, forced to quit his life as an astronaut, hounded by the news media, tortured in public wherever he goes.

This is where we see what the protagonist is made of. Everything in the story points to the conclusion that Kinsman would be far better off to leave the priest in the wilderness to die. That is, if Kinsman makes a choice that we would consider to be morally wrong, it would be to his advantage. On the other hand, if he makes the morally correct choice and tries to save the priest, it can only result in Kinsman's downfall.

POINTS OF DECISION AND CRISIS

Every short story should reach this kind of crisis-point. This is where you, the writer, put your protagonist—and the reader!— on the needle-sharp horns of an impossibly painful dilemma. Up to this point, you have carefully convinced the reader that your protagonist is a fine and worthwhile fellow, no matter what his shortcomings and problems may be. If you have done your work well, the reader will be imagining himself as the protagonist. I wanted you to believe that you were Chet Kinsman, struggling out there on the lunar surface.

At this decision-point in the story, the writer forces the reader into an agonizing dilemma. If the protagonist chooses good instead of evil—if Kinsman saves the priest—the protagonist will surely suffer for it. If he chooses evil instead of good—if Kinsman leaves the priest to die—the protagonist will live a long and prosperous life, even though you and I know he has done a terribly wrong thing.

In a happy-ending, upbeat story, the protagonist chooses good rather than evil. He throws to the winds all that he holds dear, for the sake of doing the morally correct thing. And instead of losing all that he held dear, he comes through the fire intact. Not unscathed. The protagonist must pay some price for making the right choice. But because he made the right choice he is spared the destruction that threatened to fall upon him. Cinderella runs away from the prince, as her fairy godmother instructed her to do, yet the prince eventually finds her and they live happily ever after. Pinocchio gives up his life so that his foster father might live and gains not only life but humanity as a reward. Both of them suffered, yet they won in the end.

In a downbeat story, the protagonist deliberately chooses evil instead of good. He may gain everything he wanted, but he loses his soul; he becomes a bad person. In Faust, the protagonist literally sells his soul to the devil. He lives a long and prosperous life, but then is condemned to eternity in hell. In a more recent story, George Orwell's *1984*, the protagonist cracks under torture and gives in to the totalitarian government of Big Brother. He is rehabilitated and returned to normal society, but his freedom, his inner self, his soul—all this has been taken away from him.

There are some stories in which the protagonist makes the right choice and accomplishes what he sets out to do, but it costs him his life. This is the classic definition of tragedy. In Robert A. Heinlein's science fiction short story "The Green Hills of Earth," the blind poet Reisling makes the morally correct choice: He goes into the highly radioactive engine room of the damaged spaceship and saves the ship and its passengers from total destruction. But he dies as a result. In essence, the protagonist has traded his life for the lives of all the others on the ship. He did this knowingly and willingly. There is no nobler act that a human being can perform. This makes tragedy the highest form of storytelling, when it is written well.

"Fifteen Miles" is not a tragedy, nor is it a downbeat story.

Kinsman makes the morally correct choice. He saves the priest. Sure enough, he loses everything that he wanted to keep. This is done by implication in the story, but the implication is clear: Kinsman will be grounded, never to be an astronaut or even a flier again. He will be exposed to the public and pilloried by the media.

He will not die, of course. And in fact, he gains something of inestimable worth, something he had thought he could never find again: peace of mind. In finally letting out his secret, he loses the feelings of guilt that had been haunting him. He has become more of a man. He realizes that he can face up to whatever the world throws at him; he has come to terms with his own conscience. Instead of hiding, he is ready to take his punishment. He knows that the world cannot break his spirit. This is why the priest smiles at him at the very end of the story.

The protagonist of this story has been placed in the crucible of his own emotions and put to the fire. In "Fifteen Miles" he comes out of the fire purified, stronger than he was before he entered it.

This brings up a final point to be made about character in a short story. The protagonist must *change*. What happens to her in the course of the story, no matter how short the story may be, must change her dramatically. Where she was weak, she must become strong. Where she was evil, she must become good. (Assuming that the story is an upbeat one, of course.)

The crux of every story is the change that overcomes the protagonist. If you write a story in which the protagonist is exactly the same person at the end as at the beginning, you have a dull story on your hands. Find the point where a crucial emotional, moral and physical change happened to the protagonist.

That is what you should be writing about.

REVIEW OF THE CHARACTER CHECKLIST

Now, let us go over the points made in chapter three's checklist, in light of what I have said about "Fifteen Miles."

1. In a good story the reader forgets where he is and lives in the story; the reader wants to *be* the protagonist. "Fifteen Miles" is a heavily masculine story. The story has been widely anthologized, which means that many editors have liked it, and many readers have seen it. I suspect that most of those readers are male. That is one of the problems a writer faces: Every story choice limits your audience to some extent. When "Fifteen Miles" was written, the science fiction audience was almost 90 percent male. Today, nearly half the SF readers are women. It is certainly possible to write stories of adventure and exploration in which women are the protagonists. Yet I wonder if this particular story would work well if Kinsman were changed to a woman.

2. The protagonist must be admirable, or at least likable, but he should have at least one glaring weakness that forms the underlying tension that drives the character's behavior. Capture those conflicting traits in a simple *emotion* vs. *emotion* equation. As we have seen, Kinsman's basic equation is *guilt* vs. *duty*. I was quite clear about that before I began to write the story. He is a likable character (at least I think so) who has a remorseless weakness gnawing at his soul.

3. The protagonist must struggle to solve his problems. That struggle is the backbone of the story. Kinsman certainly struggles, both physically and emotionally. The story is a record of his struggle to deal with his various interior and exterior problems.

4. Avoid stereotypes! Kinsman is certainly not the stereotypical steely-eyed, jut-jawed hero of adventure fiction, nor is he much like the public image of NASA's astronauts. Neither Lemoyne nor Bok is a stereotype either—which leads us to the next point.

5. Study the people around you; draw your characters from life. All three of the characters in "Fifteen Miles" are based on people I have known for many years. I said above that Kinsman is not much like NASA's public relations image of its astronauts. True enough, but most of the astronauts are really not much like the public relations image that NASA has tried to maintain. Kinsman is more like a real jet-jockey: outwardly flip, inwardly torn by a moral dilemma, extremely capable in any task he undertakes. Bok and Lemoyne are, likewise, composites of people I have known, including a few Jesuits who are among the world's leading geologists.

6. Show the story from the protagonist's point of view. Every line of the story comes from Kinsman's point of view and no one else's. When he faints from exhaustion the narrative stops and resumes when he comes to. I believe that this gives the story an immediacy and emotional impact that it could not have gotten if I had shifted viewpoint among the characters, or even if I had used a more distant, godlike third-person point of view.

7. Use all five senses: Describe what your characters see, hear, touch, taste and smell. Check through the story and see where Kinsman itches, what he smells, how he strains to pull the priest out of the crevice he has fallen into. I believe the only sense I did not make use of is taste, although Bok mentions that he tasted the water melted from the ice that Father Lemoyne had unwittingly brought to their shelter.

In addition to the seven points from chapter three's checklist, there is an eighth point that came up in this chapter: The protagonist must change. Kinsman is a changed man at the end of this story. So, too, are the astronomer and the priest, though to a lesser degree.

In a well-crafted story, not only does the protagonist change, you, the writer, change also. If you put your heart and guts into what you are writing, you will not be the same person at the end of your story as you were at the beginning of it. Perhaps that is why writers have the reputation of being highly emotional; they are constantly bleeding and dying with their characters.

Chapter Six

Background in Science Fiction
Background: Theory

He was an old man who fished alone in a skiff in the Gulf Stream and he had gone eighty-four days now without taking a fish.
— *Ernest Hemingway*

In that one short opening sentence Hemingway gives you the background for his magnificent story, *The Old Man and the Sea*. Read that one sentence and you know who the story is about, where it is set, and what the old man's basic problem is.

In Victorian novels, such as Thomas Hardy's *The Mayor of Casterbridge*, it was not unusual for the author to take a whole chapter or more to lovingly draw in the background scenery for the story.

Modern readers will not sit still for such slowpaced treatment, even in a lengthy novel. In a short story the writer simply does not have the space or time to go into such detail. Yet the background can be very important to a story, especially to a science fiction story. This chapter will deal rather heavily with the particular problems that science fiction raises, although the material is applicable to all kinds of fiction.

Background is much more than mere scenery or a description of the furniture in a character's house. To a large extent, the background of a story determines the mood and color of the tale. Try to imagine Poe's "Fall of the House of Usher" set in a brightly lit supermarket, with Muzak playing constantly and infants riding around in shopping carts. Or picture O. Henry's laugh-filled "The Ransom of Red Chief" taking place in Dracula's cobwebbed castle and the surrounding Transylvanian forest!

USEFUL BACKGROUND

One of the biggest problems facing the writer of a science fiction short story is the need to create a background that is convincing without being overpowering. The writer of a contemporary story, or a historical or western or detective story, can take it for granted that the reader is familiar with most of the background details. After all, a table is a table. Modern American readers know what a stagecoach looks like; they can easily visualize the glittering chandeliers of Louis XIV's palace at Versailles; and they think they know what the inside of a jail looks like.

But what does the reader know of the ammonia seas of Titan, the largest moon of the planet Saturn? How can a reader visualize the flight deck of an interstellar spacecraft? Or the weightless recreation room of a space station, where the crew works out by playing zero-gravity volleyball?

In each and every science fiction story, the entire background must be supplied to the reader. The writer cannot say, "You know what I mean," when he mentions a laser handgun, even though he could simply use the word pistol in a western or detective story and the reader would instantly know what he meant.

This is one reason why science fiction short stories are so difficult to do well, and why science fiction is such a good discipline for any writer.

Often, the writer will start out to produce a short story and end up with a novelette—about 20,000 words instead of 5,000 to 7,000—because she needed the extra wordage to draw a convincing background.

Ten thousand words or more just for the background? This is perfectly all right, if the background is interesting and if it plays an integral part in the story's development. For example, in Orson Scott Card's famous *Ender's Game*, the entire story depends on the reader's understanding of the high-tech war games that Ender Wiggins and the other children are forced to play. Card spent much time and energy describing those games, not only because they are fascinating in their own right, but because they are vital to the unfolding of the story Card wants to tell.

On the other hand, there have been many science fiction stories in which the background has taken over the entire story and pushed everything else into obscurity. Such stories are usually quite dull. A strange, alien, exotic world may seem exciting, but people want to read about people and not about inanimate objects, no matter how fascinating they may be. A story is about people; take out the people and you have a travelogue, at best.

Of course, a good writer can break that rule (or any other) and get away with it. Isaac Asimov's classic short story "The Last Question" starts with a couple of human characters, but they exist merely to ask of a supercomputer, "Can anything prevent the end of the universe?" The story then leaps forward millions of years at a time. Human characters disappear, only larger and more complex computers people the tale, until at last a computer so vast that it extends beyond the visible universe comes up with the answer to the question. This intellectual exercise can hardly be called a story: It violates all the rules of commercial fiction, yet it remains an intriguing and enduring masterpiece and was Asimov's favorite among all the stories he wrote.

There are other good stories in which no human being appears, and at first glance they seem to be nothing but background, with no plot or characters at all. But look at Ray Bradbury's "There Will Come Soft Rains." On the surface, it is the story of a completely automated house slowly falling into ruin. Look deeper. That house is itself a character, and it goes through all the phases of life (and death) that the humans did when they lived in it.

Although many writers find that they must devote about as many words to the background of a science fiction story as they do to the main line of the story itself, there are others who prefer to sketch in the background very lightly and depend on the reader's imagination to fill in the details. These writers concentrate on the fictional aspects of the story—the characters and conflict—and leave the background pretty much alone.

It is especially tempting to tell yourself that science fiction readers already know, roughly, what a laser handgun is. Or that so many people have seen "Star Trek" or other "sci-fi" movies in which starships use hyperdrive to exceed the speed of light that there is no need to give any details about such fictitious concepts.

This can be a very dangerous attitude. At the very least, it can lead to stories that are filled with jargon such as space warp, psionics, antigravs, droids and such. These may save space, but they also restrict the understanding of the story for everyone except the hard-core science fiction readers.

Worse still, they usually show that the writer has not been very original. By using the standard jargon of science fiction, you just might find yourself wallowing in the standard clichés, as well. It may be perfectly permissible to tread the same ground again and again in westerns or detective stories, but in science fiction, where you have the whole universe and all of time as your playground, the audience demands freshness and originality. Yes, I know, there are dull stories published that use those clichés and trot out those bits of jargon again and again. But this is merely proof of Sturgeon's Law, coined many years ago by one of the best science fiction writers, Theodore Sturgeon: "Ninety-five percent of science fiction is crud; but then, ninety-five percent of *everything* is crud."

You want to be in the good 5 percent! So beware of shortcut jargon and short-circuited thinking.

This is not to say that you should spend page after page trying to describe how a thermonuclear fusion rocket works, especially since there is no such device as yet, and your description is apt to be largely phony. Sternly resist the temptation to show the reader how much science you know (or how many reference books you have read) by piling on detailed explanations of scientific matters.

MAKING BACKGROUND WORK

All right, then, how does a writer make an effective, fascinating background for a short story without going into excruciating detail? Here are a few simple guidelines.

1. Make every background detail work. That is, everything about the background should be important to the story. In a short story you do not have the room, and the reader does not have the time, to rhapsodize over multicolored sunsets on a planet that has six suns. Not unless those gorgeous colors will affect the outcome of the story! If it is in the story merely for the sake of exotic detail, or simply because you enjoyed writing that paragraph, take it out. Only those background details that affect the story's development and resolution should be in your final draft. Even in a novel, where you have room and time to be more expansive, beware of details that do not add to the story's flow. It is easy to get sidetracked, very difficult to get back into the main flow of your story once you have drifted away from it.

2. Do not try to explain how the machinery works; just show what it does. Fifty years ago, science fiction writers went into painstaking detail to show the reader that gyroscopes really could be used to maneuver a spacecraft on its way to the moon. Today such explanations are laughable, even though they're technically quite correct, because spacecraft do not use gyroscopes for altitude control; gas jets are lighter, smaller and more reliable.

Today's reader is perfectly willing to accept that modern technology can make just about anything possible. You do not need to explain how a fusion reactor works; such an explanation would slow up the story. To convince your readers that a fusion reactor exists, so that they will accept that part of your story, describe a bit of the machine's external appearance and tell the reader what it does:

> The lasers that powered the fusion reactor were a lot smaller than Jean had expected. Small, but powerful. The reactor chamber itself was nothing more than a rounded metal dome, gleaming dully in the overhead lights. But the gauges on the power board told the real story: The reactor was turning out enough power—noiselessly—to light the entire city.

3. Feel free to invent any new devices, to make any new scientific discoveries that you can imagine—providing they do not contradict what is known about science today. This is a bit tricky, because to some extent any new scientific discovery is bound to contradict some aspect of known science. But science fiction readers love to play The Game, as it is called. They carefully scrutinize each story, looking for scientific or technological errors. Did you ever count the shots that Hopalong Cassidy made with his six-shooter without reloading? Science fiction readers are much more meticulous than that.

For example, it is perfectly all right to do a story in which there are microscopic living creatures on Mars. None has been discovered so far, but no one can yet say that Mars is totally devoid of life. But if you try to depict those Martians as oxygen breathers, the science fiction readers will raise a howl of protest. Our space probes of Mars, such as the *Viking* landers, have shown conclusively that there is not enough oxygen in Mars's atmosphere to support oxygen-breathing life.

Decades ago, the science fiction audience was perfectly content to accept stories in which Mars was crisscrossed by canals dug by intelligent Martians. Even though the best astronomical researchers stoutly maintained that the Martian canals were only optical illusions, the science fiction readers remained open-minded on the subject. Besides, Mars with canals seemed much more interesting than Mars without canals. But when spacecraft photographs proved that there were no canals on Mars, no writer could ever again do a science fiction story that had Martian canals in it. The audience would no longer accept it.

The point is that science fiction has some affinity with science. And while the science fiction audience is much more open-minded about the future than any professional scientist, they will still turn against stories that betray an ignorance or disdain of accepted scientific fact.

You can write stories in which Mars is spiderwebbed with canals. Or stories in which elephants fly, for that matter. But they will not be accepted by the science fiction audience as science fiction. They may be published, read and enjoyed as SF or fantasy. But if you are trying to write *science* fiction, you will have to know the basics of scientific understanding. And if you break any of the fundamental laws of science, you had better have an excellent explanation for it!

4. You should be thoroughly familiar with the background of your story. In other words, write about what you know. A writer whose only contact with the Pentagon is from reading other stories or watching movies will have a very difficult time writing convincingly about the Joint Chiefs of Staff, because he has not found out how these people talk, think or act. I have seen manuscript after manuscript in which the writer is trying to deal with situations and backgrounds that he knows absolutely nothing about. Such manuscripts go from the slushpile to return mail, usually with nothing more than a standard rejection notice on them.

No one has been to Mars, yet, although NASA has provided us with fascinating photographs of the Red Planet, both from orbit and from the *Viking* landers that have been sitting on the red soil of Mars since 1976. But long before the first *Mariner* spacecraft was even designed, Edgar Rice Burroughs, Stanley G. Weinbaum, Ray Bradbury and many others wrote stories about Mars. They were not writing out of firsthand experience at all.

Or were they? These writers took pains to acquire as much information about Mars as they could. Then they built up a world in their own imagination that did not contradict what was known about Mars and filled in the unknown areas with creations of their own mind.

In a sense, each of them built a new world inside his head, loosely based on what was known about Mars at that time. Thus, Burroughs created the exotic Barsoom of John Carter, master swordsman; Weinbaum created the desert world populated by strangely nonhuman Martians; and Bradbury created a fantasy world of bone-chess cities and telepathic, very human, Martian men and women.

None of these imaginary worlds could be written about today and still be called Mars. We know too much about Mars now; each of these imaginary worlds contradicts the pitiless advance of knowledge. But a writer can still create such imaginary worlds and place them around another star. That would not contradict real-world knowledge, and the universe is vast enough to justify almost any kind of world.

This advance of knowledge is a two-edged sword. On one hand, it makes it increasingly difficult to get away with ideas that run counter to scientific knowledge.

On the other hand, the advance of knowledge means that writers have more information on which to base stories. It is now possible to write extremely realistic stories about living and working on the moon. My novel *Mars* was written with the benefit of exact knowledge of the landscape, the weather, and the other physical conditions of the Martian surface. We know in fine detail how nuclear reactors work, what the bottom of the ocean is like, how the double-helix molecule of DNA carries genetic information from one generation to the next.

You must write about what you know. And what you know is a combination of hard information from the world around you, plus that special interior world of imagination that is yours and yours alone until you share it with your audience.

In short, be certain that you have the factual information you need to make your story authentic, but don't let that stifle your imagination. It is your imaginative handling of the facts that makes the difference between a dull scientific treatise and a thrilling science fiction adventure.

5. (This pointer is actually a corollary to the fourth.) It is important to learn the basics of science. The task is not difficult; in fact, it can be very exciting. Most science fiction writers are interested in science to some degree, although a good many of them are turned off by school classes in physics, chemistry or math.

One of the best ways I know to learn about science on your own and at your own pace is to read the popularized science books that are published each year. When I started writing, Isaac Asimov and Arthur C. Clarke were the only two reliable writers of science for the general audience. Thanks to their success, publishers began to see that there was a profitable audience for nonfiction books about science. In 1978, *Omni* magazine began to show that millions of interested men and women would read a science-oriented magazine every month. Today, there are so many science books published every month that I write a quarterly book review column for *The Hartford Courant* specifically on science books.

Science is beautiful, and anyone can understand the basics of scientific thought. Poets who sing about the eternal beauty of the stars without understanding what makes them shine and how they were created are missing more than half of the real splendor of the heavens.

6. Equally important to the setting and scenery of a story is the care used in naming people, places and things. Names are important; they help set the tone for a story.

The reader would have a tough time imagining a two-fisted hero named Elmer Small, but Jame Retief comes across just fine as a hero in Keith Laumer's stories. Similarly, Bubbles La Toure is hardly the name of a saintly nun, whereas Modesty Blaise is a sexy and intriguing name for a female counterpart of James Bond.

Science fiction names should be familiar enough to be understood without fumbling over them. Yet frequently a name has to convey the alienness of a person or a locale. Too often, new writers lapse into unpronounceable collections of letters, such as Brfstklb. It's unusual, all right, but every time the readers see it, they will balk at such a name and stop reading. The break may be only momentary, but any break in reading a story can be fatal.

Maps are a good place to find strange names, provided you are careful to use names that are unfamiliar, yet have an interesting ring about them. It is often useful to take a place name and give it to a person. The heroine of a novel of mine was named Altai, after the high, wild mountain chain in western China. Also, there is history to draw from: Larry Niven's character Beowulf Schaffer is fascinating even before you've met him.

One important rule of thumb about names: If a name makes the reader giggle, get rid of it unless it is a giggle that you are seeking. Be ruthless about this. Nothing ruins a story faster than an unintentionally humorous name.

7. The story must be internally consistent. This is much more than a matter of keeping track of what time it is and which way the wind was blowing in the last scene.

In a science fiction story, where the background forms an important element of the total story line, the background itself must be internally consistent. The writer cannot change winter to summer overnight because he wants a scene set on a sweltering day. More importantly, he cannot tamper with the laws of nature to suit the needs of the story.

The archetype of this requirement is Tom Godwin's "The Cold Equations," in which the laws of nature are the background of the story.

In this story, a young woman stows away on a spaceship carrying desperately needed vaccine to a plague-stricken planet. She wants to reach her brother, who is one of the plague victims. The ship's pilot, its only crew member, discovers the stowaway and realizes that her extra weight will prevent the ship from reaching its destination. He decides that the lives of millions of plague victims outweigh the life of the stowaway, and forces her out of the airlock, to die in the vacuum of space.

A cold equation had been balanced and he was alone on the ship. . . . It seemed, almost, that she still sat small and bewildered and frightened on the metal box beside him, her words echoing hauntingly clear in the void she had left behind her:

I didn't do anything to die for—I didn't do anything—

The theme of the story is classical: The universe (or what the ancient Greeks would have called Destiny) does not care about our petty loves and desires. One and one inexorably add up to two, no matter how desperately we would have it otherwise.

Godwin could have pulled a last-minute switch and had the pilot invent some nifty device that would save both the woman and the dying plague victims. But that would have ruined the story's dramatic impact, especially since he set out to show that there are forces of nature that cannot be appeased by human desires.

When you have an explorer lost on a new planet in a sandstorm that will go on for a month, you had better make certain that the storm does not stop for a full thirty days. Otherwise, the reader will realize that the author has artificially helped his protagonist, and the reader will reject the story—if it gets published at all.

Keep in mind that old phrase, "It's too good to be true." Readers will not accept lucky breaks that help the protagonist; they will regard such good fortune as author manipulation. Even the redoubtable Charles Dickens has been faulted for the fortunate coincidences that often save his characters from cruel fates. On the other hand, there is no such phrase as "It's too *bad* to be true." Readers will accept just about any calamity that you want to pile onto your protagonist. Just look at the Book of Job, for example!

Backgrounds must be consistent in all aspects, even the mundane, undramatic ones. It makes no sense to depict a desperate society that has depleted all its energy-producing fuels, yet has a government that watches all its citizens over closed-circuit television. Where would the government get the fuel? Not merely the fuel to provide electricity for their electronic snooping, but the fuel that it takes to build and maintain all this widespread equipment?

And some slightly deeper thinking might lead you to the conclusion that an energy-poor civilization would not have as large a population as a modern industrial society. Nor would the population density be as high. A *1984*-type of government would be extremely unlikely in a world that resembled the medieval subsistence farming societies of A.D. 1284.

Even though science fiction writers can bend the rules if they want to, it is best to think long and hard about it beforehand. The background of a science fiction story is so important that it often shapes the path that the story takes, just as the environment around us shapes our behavior. Pay attention to the background and avoid the hackneyed territory that has been so overrun by mediocre stories.

Set your stories in your unique world, guided—but not hamstrung—by known scientific information.

A BACKGROUND CHECKLIST

To recapitulate the major points of this chapter:

1. Make every background detail work.

2. Don't try to explain how the machinery works; just show what it does.

3. Feel free to invent any new devices or scientific discoveries that you can imagine—providing they do not contradict what is known about science today.

4. Be thoroughly familiar with the background of your story.

5. Learn the basics of science.

6. Names are important.

7. The background—and the story itself—must be internally consistent.

Chapter Seven

Background in Science Fiction

Sepulcher

A Complete Short Story

I was a soldier," he said. "Now I am a priest. You may call me Dorn."

Elverda Apacheta could not help staring at him. She had seen cyborgs before, but this . . . person seemed more machine than man. She felt a chill ripple of contempt along her veins. How could a human being allow his body to be disfigured so?

He was not tall; Elverda herself stood several centimeters taller than he. His shoulders were quite broad, though; his torso thick and solid. The left side of his face was engraved metal, as was the entire top of his head: like a skullcap made of finest etched steel.

Dorn's left hand was prosthetic. He made no attempt to disguise it. Beneath the rough fabric of his shabby tunic and threadbare trousers, how much more of him was metal and electrical machinery? Tattered though his clothing was, his calf-length boots were polished to a high gloss.

"A priest?" asked Miles Sterling. "Of what church? What order?"

The half of Dorn's lips that could move made a slight curl. A smile or a sneer, Elverda could not tell.

"I will show you to your quarters," said Dorn. His voice was a low rumble, as if it came from the belly of a beast. It echoed faintly off the walls of rough-hewn rock.

Sterling looked briefly surprised. He was not accustomed to having his questions ignored. Elverda watched his face. Sterling was as handsome as cosmetic surgery could make a person appear: chiseled features, earnest sky-blue eyes, straight of spine, long of limb, athletically flat midsection. Yet there was a faint smell of corruption about him, Elverda thought. As if he were dead inside and already beginning to rot.

The tension between the two men seemed to drain the energy from Elverda's aged body. "It has been a long journey," she said. "I am very tired. I would welcome a hot shower and a long nap."

"Before you see it?" Sterling snapped.

"It has taken us months to get here. We can wait a few hours more." Inwardly she marvelled at her own words. Once she would have been all fiery excitement. Have the years taught you patience? No, she realized. Only weariness.

"Not me!" Sterling said. Turning to Dorn, "Take me to it now. I've waited long enough. I want to see it now."

Dorn's eyes, one as brown as Elverda's own, the other a red electronic glow, regarded Sterling for a lengthening moment.

"Well?" Sterling demanded.

"I am afraid, sir, that the chamber is sealed for the next twelve hours. It will be imposs—"

"Sealed? By whom? On whose authority?"

"The chamber is self-controlled. Whoever made the artifact installed the controls, as well."

"No one told me about that," said Sterling.

Dorn replied, "Your quarters are down this corridor."

He turned almost like a solid block of metal, shoulders and hips together, head unmoving on those wide shoulders, and started down the central corridor. Elverda fell in step alongside his metal half, still angered at his self-desecration. Yet despite herself, she thought of what a challenge it would be to sculpt him. If I were younger, she told herself. If I were not so close to death. Human and inhuman, all in one strangely fierce figure.

Sterling came up on Dorn's other side, his face red with barely suppressed anger.

They walked down the corridor in silence, Sterling's weighted shoes clicking against the uneven rock floor. Dorn's boots made hardly any noise at all. Half-machine he may be, Elverda thought, but once in motion he moves like a panther.

The asteroid's inherent gravity was so slight that Sterling needed the weighted footgear to keep himself from stumbling ridiculously. Elverda, who had spent most of her long life in low-gravity environments, felt completely at home. The corridor they were walking through was actually a tunnel, shadowy and mysterious, or perhaps a natural chimney vented through the rocky body by escaping gases eons ago when the asteroid was still molten. Now it was cold, chill enough to make Elverda shudder. The rough ceiling was so low she wanted to stoop, even though the rational side of her mind knew it was not necessary.

Soon, though, the walls smoothed out and the ceiling grew higher. Humans had extended the tunnel, squaring it with laser precision. Doors lined both walls now and the ceiling glowed with glareless, shadowless light. Still she hugged herself against the chill that the others did not seem to notice.

They stopped at a wide double door. Dorn tapped out the entrance code on the panel set into the wall and the doors slid open.

"Your quarters, sir," he said to Sterling. "You may, of course, change the privacy code to suit yourself."

Sterling gave a curt nod and strode through the open doorway. Elverda got a glimpse of a spacious suite, carpeting on the floor and hologram windows on the walls.

Sterling turned in the doorway to face them. "I expect you to call for me in twelve hours," he said to Dorn, his voice hard.

"Eleven hours and fifty-seven minutes," Dorn replied.

Sterling's nostrils flared and he slid the double doors shut.

"This way." Dorn gestured with his human hand. "I'm afraid your quarters are not as sumptuous as Mr. Sterling's."

Elverda said, "I am his guest. He is paying all the bills."

"You are a great artist. I have heard of you."

"Thank you."

"For the truth? That is not necessary."

I was a great artist, Elverda said to herself. Once. Long ago. Now I am an old woman waiting for death. Aloud, she asked, "Have you seen my work?"

Dorn's voice grew heavier. "Only holograms. Once I set out to see *The Rememberer* for myself, but — other matters intervened."

"You were a soldier then?"

"Yes. I have been a priest only since coming to this place."

Elverda wanted to ask him more, but Dorn stopped before a blank door and opened it for her. For an instant she thought he was going to reach for her with his prosthetic hand. She shrank away from him.

"I will call for you in eleven hours and fifty-six minutes," he said, as if he had not noticed her revulsion.

"Thank you."

He turned away, like a machine pivoting.

"Wait," Elverda called. "Please — How many others are here? Everything seems so quiet."

"There are no others. Only the three of us."

"But — "

"I am in charge of the security brigade. I ordered the others of my command to go back to our spacecraft and wait there."

"And the scientists? The prospector family that found this asteroid?"

"They are in Mr. Sterling's spacecraft, the one you arrived in," said Dorn. "Under the protection of my brigade."

Elverda looked into his eyes. Whatever burned in them, she could not fathom.

"Then we are alone here?"

Dorn nodded solemnly. "You and me — and Mr. Sterling, who pays all the bills." The human half of his face remained as immobile as the metal. Elverda could not tell if he was trying to be humorous or bitter.

"Thank you," she said. He turned away and she closed the door.

Her quarters consisted of a single room, comfortably warm but hardly larger than the compartment on the ship they had come in. Elverda saw that her meager travel bag was already sitting on the bed, her worn old drawing computer resting in its travel-smudged case on the desk. Elverda stared at the computer case as if it were accusing her. I should have left it home, she thought. I will never use it again.

A small utility robot, hardly more than a glistening drum of metal and six gleaming arms folded like a praying mantis's, stood mutely in the farthest corner. Elverda stared at it. At least it was entirely a machine; not a self-mutilated human being. To take the most beautiful form in the universe and turn it into a hybrid mechanism, a travesty of humanity. Why did he do it? So he could be a better soldier? A more efficient killing machine?

And why did he send all the others away? she asked herself while she opened the travel bag. As she carried her toiletries to the narrow alcove of the bathroom, a new thought struck her.

Did he send them away before he saw the artifact, or afterward? Has he even seen it? Perhaps. . . .

Then she saw her reflection in the mirror above the wash basin. Her heart sank. Once she had been called regal, stately, a goddess made of copper. Now she looked withered, dried up, bone thin, her face a geological map of too many years of living, her flight coveralls hanging limply on her emaciated frame.

You are old, she said to her image. Old and aching and tired.

It is the long trip, she told herself. You need to rest. But the other voice in her mind laughed scornfully. You've done nothing but rest for the entire time it's taken to reach this piece of rock. You are ready for the permanent rest; why deny it?

She had been teaching at the university on Luna, the closest she could get to Earth after a long lifetime of living in low-gravity environments. Close enough to see the world of her birth, the only world of life and warmth in the solar system, the only place where a person could walk out in the sunshine and feel its warmth soaking your bones, smell the fertile earth nurturing its bounty, feel a cool breeze plucking at your hair.

But she had separated herself from Earth permanently. She had stood at the shore of Titan's methane sea; from an orbiting spacecraft she had watched the surging clouds of Jupiter swirl their overpowering colors; she had carved the kilometer-long rock of *The Rememberer*. But she could no longer stand in the village of her birth, at the edge of the Pacific's booming surf, and watch the soft white clouds form shapes of imaginary animals.

Her creative life was long finished. She had lived too long; there were no friends left, and she had never had a family. There was no purpose to her life, no reason to do anything except go through the motions and wait. At the university she was no longer truly working at her art but helping students who had the fires of inspiration burning fresh and hot inside them. Her life was one of vain regrets for all the things she had not accomplished, for all the failures she could recall. Failures at love; those were the bitterest. She was praised as the solar system's greatest artist: the sculptress of *The Rememberer*, the creator of the first great ionospheric painting, *The Virgin of the Andes*. She was respected, but not loved. She felt empty, alone, barren. She had nothing to look forward to; absolutely nothing.

Then Miles Sterling swept into her existence. A lifetime

younger, bold, vital, even ruthless, he stormed her academic tower with the news that an alien artifact had been discovered deep in the asteroid belt.

"It's some kind of art form," he said, desperate with excitement. "You've got to come with me and see it."

Trying to control the long-forgotten longing that stirred within her, Elverda had asked quietly, "Why do I have to go with you, Mr. Sterling? Why me? I'm an old wo—"

"You are the greatest artist of our time," he had snapped. "You've *got* to see this! Don't bullshit me with false modesty. You're the only other person in the whole whirling solar system who *deserves* to see it!"

"The only other person besides whom?" she had asked.

He had blinked with surprise. "Why, besides me, of course."

So now we are on this nameless asteroid, waiting to see the alien artwork. Just the three of us. The richest man in the solar system. An elderly artist who has outlived her usefulness. And a cyborg soldier who has cleared everyone else away.

He claims to be a priest, Elverda remembered. A priest who is half machine. She shivered as if a cold wind surged through her.

A harsh buzzing noise interrupted her thoughts. Looking into the main part of the room, Elverda saw that the phone screen was blinking red in rhythm to the buzzing.

"Phone," she called out.

Sterling's face appeared on the screen instantly. "Come to my quarters," he said. "We have to talk."

"Give me an hour. I need—"

"Now."

Elverda felt her brows rise haughtily. Then the strength sagged out of her. He has bought the right to command you, she told herself. He is quite capable of refusing to allow you to see the artifact.

"Now," she agreed.

Sterling was pacing across the plush carpeting when she arrived at his quarters. He had changed from his flight coveralls to a comfortably loose royal blue pullover and expensive genuine twill slacks. As the doors slid shut behind her, he stopped in front of a low couch and faced her squarely.

"Do you know who this Dorn creature is?"

Elverda answered, "Only what he has told us."

"I've checked him out. My staff in the ship has a complete file on him. He's the butcher who led the *Chrysalis* massacre, fourteen years ago."

"He . . ."

"Eleven hundred men, women and children. Slaughtered. He was the man who commanded the attack."

"He said he had been a soldier."

"A mercenary. A cold-blooded murderer. He was working for Toyama then. The *Chrysalis* was their habitat. When its population voted for independence, Toyama put him in charge of a squad to bring them back into line. He killed them all; turned off their air and let them all die."

Elverda felt shakily for the nearest chair and sank into it. Her legs seemed to have lost all their strength.

"His name was Harbin then. Dorik Harbin."

"Wasn't he brought to trial?"

"No. He ran away. Disappeared. I always thought Toyama helped to hide him. They take care of their own, they do. He must have changed his name afterwards. Nobody would hire the butcher, not even Toyama."

"His face . . . half his body . . ." Elverda felt terribly weak, almost faint. "When . . . ?"

"Must have been after he ran away. Maybe it was an attempt to disguise himself."

"And now he is working for you." She wanted to laugh at the irony of it, but did not have the strength.

"He's got us trapped on this chunk of rock! There's nobody else here except the three of us."

"You have your staff in your ship. Surely they would come if you summoned them."

"His security squad's been ordered to keep everybody except you and me off the asteroid. He gave those orders."

"You can countermand them, can't you?"

For the first time since she had met Miles Sterling, he looked unsure of himself. "I wonder," he said.

"Why?" Elverda asked. "Why is he doing this?"

"That's what I intend to find out." Sterling strode to the phone console. "Harbin!" he called. "Dorik Harbin. Come to my quarters at once."

Without even an eyeblink's delay the phone's computer-synthesized voice replied, "Dorik Harbin no longer exists. Transferring your call to Dorn."

Sterling's blue eyes snapped at the phone's blank screen.

"Dorn is not available at present," the phone's voice said. "He will call for you in eleven hours and thirty-two minutes."

"God-*damn* it!" Sterling smacked a fist into the open palm of his other hand. "Get me the officer on watch aboard the *Sterling Eagle*."

"All exterior communications are inoperable at the present time," replied the phone.

"That's impossible!"

"All exterior communications are inoperable at the present time," the phone repeated, unperturbed.

Sterling stared at the empty screen, then turned slowly toward Elverda. "He's cut us off. We're really trapped here."

Elverda felt the chill of cold metal clutching at her. Perhaps Dorn is a madman, she thought. Perhaps he is my death, personified.

"We've got to do something!" Sterling nearly shouted.

Elverda rose shakily to her feet. "There is nothing that we can do, for the moment. I am going to my quarters and take a nap. I believe that Dorn, or Harbin or whatever his identity is, will call on us when he is ready to."

"And do what?"

"Show us the artifact," she replied, silently adding, I hope.

Legally, the artifact and the entire asteroid belonged to Sterling Enterprises, Ltd. It had been discovered by a family—husband, wife and two sons, ages five and three—that made a living from searching out iron-nickel asteroids and selling the mining rights to the big corporations. They filed their claim to this unnamed asteroid, together with a preliminary description of its ten-kilometer-wide shape, its orbit within the asteroid belt, and a sample analysis of its surface composition.

Six hours after their original transmission reached the commodities market computer network on Earth—while a fairly spirited bidding was going on among four major corporations for the asteroid's mineral rights—a new message arrived at the headquarters of the International Astronautical Authority, in London. The message was garbled, fragmentary, obviously made in great haste and at fever excitement. There was an artifact of some sort in a cavern deep inside the asteroid.

One of the faceless bureaucrats buried deep within the IAA's multilayered organization sent an immediate message to an employee of Sterling Enterprises, Ltd. The bureaucrat retired hours later, richer than he had any right to expect, while Miles Sterling personally contacted the prospectors and bought the asteroid outright for enough money to end their prospecting days forever. By the time the decision-makers in the IAA realized that an alien artifact had been discovered, they were faced with a fait accompli: The artifact, and the asteroid in which it resided, were the personal property of the richest man in the solar system.

Miles Sterling was no egomaniac. Nor was he a fool. Graciously he allowed the IAA to organize a team of scientists who would inspect this first specimen of alien existence. Even more graciously, Sterling offered to ferry the scientific investigators all the long way to the asteroid at his own expense. He made only one demand, and the IAA could hardly refuse him. He insisted that he see this artifact himself before the scientists were allowed to view it.

And he brought along the solar system's most honored and famous artist. To appraise the artifact's worth as an art object, he claimed. To determine how much he could deduct from his corporate taxes by donating the thing to the IAA, said his enemies. But over the months of their voyage to the asteroid, Elverda came to the conclusion that buried deep beneath his ruthless business persona was an eager little boy who was tremendously excited at having found a new toy. A toy he intended to possess for himself. An art object, created by alien hands.

For an art object was what the artifact seemed to be. The family of prospectors continued to send back vague, almost irrational reports of what the artifact looked like. The reports were worthless. No two descriptions matched. If the man and woman were to be believed, the artifact did nothing but sit in the middle of a rough-hewn cavern. But they described it differently with every report they sent. It glowed with light. It was darker than deep space. It was a statue of some sort. It was formless. It overwhelmed the senses. It was small enough almost to pick up in one hand. It made the children laugh happily. It frightened their parents. When they tried to photograph it, their transmissions showed nothing but blank screens. Totally blank.

As Sterling listened to their maddening reports and waited impatiently for the IAA to organize its hand-picked team of scientists, he ordered his security manager to get a squad of hired personnel to the asteroid as quickly as possible. From corporate facilities on Titan and the moons of Mars, from three separate outposts among the asteroid belt itself, Sterling Enterprises efficiently brought together a brigade of experienced mercenary security troops. They reached the asteroid long before anyone else could, and were under orders to make certain that no one was allowed onto the asteroid before Miles Sterling himself reached it.

"The time has come."

Elverda woke slowly, painfully, like a swimmer struggling for the air and light of the surface. She had been dreaming of her childhood, of the village where she had grown up, the distant snow-capped Andes, the warm night breezes that spoke of love.

"The time has come."

It was Dorn's deep voice, whisper-soft. Startled, she flashed her eyes open. She was alone in the room, but Dorn's image filled the phone screen by her bed. The numbers glowing beneath the screen showed that it was indeed time.

"I am awake now," she said to the screen.

"I will be at your door in fifteen minutes," Dorn said. "Will that be enough time for you to prepare yourself?"

"Yes, plenty." The days when she needed time for selecting her clothing and arranging her appearance were long gone.

"In fifteen minutes, then."

"Wait," she blurted. "Can you see me?"

"No. Visual transmission must be keyed manually."

"I see."

"I do not."

A joke? Elverda sat up on the bed as Dorn's image winked out. Is he capable of humor?

She shrugged out of the shapeless coveralls she had worn to bed, took a quick shower, and pulled her best caftan from the travel bag. It was a deep midnight blue, scattered with glittering silver stars. Elverda had made the floor-length gown herself, from fabric woven by her mother long ago. She had painted the stars from her memory of what they had looked like from her native village.

As she slid back her front door she saw Dorn marching down the corridor with Sterling beside him. Despite his longer legs, Sterling seemed to be scampering like a child to keep up with Dorn's steady, stolid steps.

"I *demand* that you reinstate communications with my ship," Sterling was saying, his voice echoing off the corridor walls. "I'll dock your pay for every minute this insubordination continues!"

"It is a security measure," Dorn said calmly, without turning to look at the man. "It is for your own good."

"My own good? Who in hell are you to determine what my own good might be?"

Dorn stopped three paces short of Elverda, made a stiff little bow to her, and only then turned to face his employer.

"Sir: I have seen the artifact. You have not."

"And that makes you better than me?" Sterling almost snarled the words. "Holier, maybe?"

"No," said Dorn. "Not holier. Wiser."

Sterling started to reply, then thought better of it.

"Which way do we go?" Elverda asked in the sudden silence.

Dorn pointed with his prosthetic hand. "Down," he replied. "This way."

The corridor abruptly became a rugged tunnel again, with lights fastened at precisely spaced intervals along the low ceiling. Elverda watched Dorn's half-human face as the pools of shadow chased the highlights glinting off the etched metal, like the Moon racing through its phases every half-minute, over and again.

Sterling had fallen silent as they followed the slanting tunnel downward into the heart of the rock. Elverda heard only the clicking of his shoes, at first, but by concentrating she was able to make out the softer footfalls of Dorn's padded boots and even the whisper of her own slippers.

The air seemed to grow warmer, closer. Or is it my own anticipation? She glanced at Sterling; perspiration beaded his upper lip. The man radiated tense expectation. Dorn glided a few steps ahead of them. He did not seem to be hurrying, yet he was now leading them down the tunnel, like an ancient priest leading two new acolytes—or sacrificial victims.

The tunnel ended in a smooth wall of dull metal.

"We are here."

"Open it up," Sterling demanded.

"It will open itself," replied Dorn. He waited a heartbeat, then added, "Now."

And the metal slid up into the rock above them as silently as if it were a curtain made of silk.

None of them moved. Then Dorn slowly turned toward the two of them and gestured with his human hand.

"The artifact lies twenty-two point nine meters beyond this point. The tunnel narrows and turns to the right. The chamber is large enough to accommodate only one person at a time, comfortably."

"Me first!" Sterling took a step forward.

Dorn stopped him with an upraised hand. The prosthetic hand. "I feel it my duty to caution you—"

Sterling tried to push the hand away; he could not budge it.

"When I first crossed this line, I was a soldier. After I saw the artifact I gave up my life."

"And became a self-styled priest. So what?"

"The artifact can change you. I thought it best that there be no witnesses to your first viewing of it, except for this gifted woman whom you have brought with you. When you first see it, it can be—traumatic."

Sterling's face twisted with a mixture of anger and disgust. "I'm not a mercenary killer. I don't have anything to be afraid of."

Dorn let his hand drop to his side with a faint whine of miniaturized servomotors.

"Perhaps not," he murmured, so low that Elverda barely heard it.

Sterling shouldered his way past the cyborg. "Stay here," he told Elverda. "You can see it when I come back."

He hurried down the tunnel, footsteps staccato.

Then silence.

Elverda looked at Dorn. The human side of his face seemed utterly weary.

"You have seen the artifact more than once, haven't you?"

"Fourteen times," he answered.

"It has not harmed you in any way, has it?"

He hesitated, then replied, "It has changed me. Each time I see it, it changes me more."

"You . . . you really are Dorik Harbin?"

"I was."

"Those people of the *Chrysalis* . . . ?"

"Dorik Harbin killed them all. Yes. There is no excuse for it, no pardon. It was the act of a monster."

"But why?"

"Monsters do monstrous things. Dorik Harbin ingested psychotropic drugs to increase his battle prowess. Afterward, when the battle drugs cleared from his bloodstream and he understood what he had done, Dorik Harbin held a grenade against his chest and set it off."

"Oh my god," Elverda whimpered.

"He was not allowed to die, however. The medical specialists rebuilt his body and he was given a false identity. For many years he lived a sham of life, hiding from the authorities, hiding from his own guilt. He no longer had the courage to kill himself; the pain of his first attempt was far stronger than his own self-loathing. Then he was hired to come to this place. Dorik Harbin looked upon the artifact for the first time, and his true identity emerged at last."

Elverda heard a scuffling sound, like feet dragging, staggering. Miles Sterling came into view, tottering, leaning heavily against the wall of the tunnel, slumping as if his legs could no longer hold him.

"No man . . . no one. . . ." He pushed himself forward and collapsed into Dorn's arms.

"Destroy it!" he whispered harshly, spittle dribbling down his chin. "Destroy this whole damned piece of rock! Wipe it out of existence!"

"What is it?" Elverda asked. "What did you see?"

Dorn lowered him to the ground gently. Sterling's feet scrabbled against the rock as if he were trying to run away. Sweat covered his face, soaked his shirt.

"It's . . . beyond . . ." he babbled. "More . . . than anyone can . . . nobody could stand it . . ."

Elverda sank to her knees beside him. "What has happened

to him?" She looked up at Dorn, who knelt on Sterling's other side.

"The artifact."

Sterling suddenly ranted, "They'll find out about me! Everyone will know! It's got to be destroyed! Nuke it! Blast it to bits!" His fists windmilled in the air, his eyes were wild.

"I tried to warn him," Dorn said as he held Sterling's shoulders down, the man's head in his lap. "I tried to prepare him for it."

"What did he see?" Elverda's heart was pounding; she could hear it thundering in her ears. "What is it? What did *you* see?"

Dorn shook his head slowly. "I cannot describe it. I doubt that anyone could describe it—except, perhaps, an artist: a person who has trained herself to see the truth."

"The prospectors—they saw it. Even their children saw it."

"Yes. When I arrived here they had spent eighteen days in the chamber. They left it only when the chamber closed itself. They ate and slept and returned here, as if hypnotized."

"It did not hurt them, did it?"

"They were emaciated, dehydrated. It took a dozen of my strongest men to remove them to my ship. Even the children fought us."

"But—how could . . ." Elverda's voice faded into silence. She looked at the brightly lit tunnel. Her breath caught in her throat.

"Destroy it," Sterling mumbled. "Destroy it before it destroys us! Don't let them find out. They'll know, they'll know, they'll all know." He began to sob uncontrollably.

"You do not have to see it," Dorn said to Elverda. "You can return to your ship and leave this place."

Leave, urged a voice inside her head. Run away. Live out what's left of your life and let it go.

Then she heard her own voice say, as if from a far distance, "I've come such a long way."

"It will change you," he warned.

"Will it release me from life?"

Dorn glanced down at Sterling, still muttering darkly, then returned his gaze to Elverda.

"It will change you," he repeated.

Elverda forced herself to her feet. Leaning one hand against the warm rock wall to steady herself, she said, "I will see it. I must."

"Yes," said Dorn. "I understand."

She looked down at him, still kneeling with Sterling's head resting in his lap. Dorn's electronic eye glowed red in the shadows. His human eye was hidden in darkness.

He said, "I believe your people say, *Vaya con Dios*."

Elverda smiled at him. She had not heard that phrase in forty years. "Yes. You too. *Vaya con Dios*." She turned and stepped across the faint groove where the metal door had met the floor.

The tunnel sloped downward only slightly. It turned sharply to the right, Elverda saw, just as Dorn had told them. The light seemed brighter beyond the turn, pulsating almost, like a living heart.

She hesitated a moment before making that final turn. What lay beyond? What difference, she answered herself. You have lived so long that you have emptied life of all its purpose. But she knew she was lying to herself. Her life was devoid of purpose because she herself had made it that way. She had spurned love; she had even rejected friendship when it had been offered. Still, she realized that she wanted to live. Desperately, she wanted to continue living no matter what.

Yet she could not resist the lure. Straightening her spine, she stepped boldly around the bend in the tunnel.

The light was so bright it hurt her eyes. She raised a hand to her brow to shield them and the intensity seemed to decrease slightly, enough to make out the faint outline of a form, a shape, a person . . .

Elverda gasped with recognition. A few meters before her, close enough to reach and touch, her mother sat on the sweet grass beneath the warm summer sun, gently rocking her baby and crooning softly to it.

Mamma! she cried silently. Mamma. The baby—Elverda herself—looked up into her mother's face and smiled.

And the mother was Elverda, a young and radiant Elverda, smiling down at the baby she had never had, tender and loving as she had never been.

Something gave way inside her. There was no pain; rather, it was as if a pain that had throbbed sullenly within her for too many years to count suddenly faded away. As if a wall of implacable ice finally melted and let the warm waters of life flow through her.

Elverda sank to the floor, crying, gushing tears of understanding and relief and gratitude. Her mother smiled at her.

"I love you, Mamma," she whispered. "I love you."

Her mother nodded and became Elverda herself once more. Her baby made a gurgling laugh of pure happiness, fat little feet waving in the air.

The image wavered, dimmed, and slowly faded into emptiness. Elverda sat on the bare rock floor in utter darkness, feeling a strange serenity and understanding warming her soul.

"Are you all right?"

Dorn's voice did not startle her. She had been expecting him to come to her.

"The chamber will close itself in another few minutes," he said. "We will have to leave."

Elverda took his offered hand and rose to her feet. She felt strong, fully in control of herself.

The tunnel outside the chamber was empty.

"Where is Sterling?"

"I sedated him and then called in a medical team to take him back to his ship."

"He wants to destroy the artifact," Elverda said.

"That will not be possible," said Dorn. "I will bring the IAA scientists here from the ship before Sterling awakes and recovers. Once they see the artifact they will not allow it to be destroyed. Sterling may own the asteroid, but the IAA will exert control over the artifact."

"The artifact will affect them—strangely."

"No two of them will be affected in the same manner," said Dorn. "And none of them will permit it to be damaged in any way."

"Sterling will not be pleased with you."

He gestured up the tunnel, and they began to walk back toward their quarters.

"Nor with you," Dorn said. "We both saw him babbling and blubbering like a baby."

"What could he have seen?"

"What he most feared. His whole life had been driven by fear, poor man."

"What secrets he must be hiding!"

"He hid them from himself. The artifact showed him his own true nature."

"No wonder he wants it destroyed."

"He cannot destroy the artifact, but he will certainly want to destroy us. Once he recovers his composure he will want to wipe out the witnesses who saw his reaction to it."

Elverda knew that Dorn was right. She watched his face as they passed beneath the lights, watched the glint of the etched metal, the warmth of the human flesh.

"You knew that he would react this way, didn't you?" she asked.

"No one could be as rich as he is without having demons driving him. He looked into his own soul and recognized himself for the first time in his life."

"You planned it this way!"

"Perhaps I did," he said. "Perhaps the artifact did it for me."

"How could—"

"It is a powerful experience. After I had seen it a few times I felt it was offering me . . . " he hesitated, then spoke the word, "salvation."

Elverda saw something in his face that Dorn had not let show before. She stopped in the shadows between overhead lights. Dorn turned to face her, half machine, standing in the rough tunnel of bare rock.

"You have had your own encounter with it," he said. "You understand now how it can transform you."

"Yes," said Elverda. "I understand."

"After a few times, I came to the realization that there must be thousands of my fellow mercenaries, killed in engagements all through the asteroid belt, still lying where they fell. Or worse yet, floating forever in space, alone, unattended, ungrieved for."

"Thousands of mercenaries?"

"The corporations do not always settle their differences in Earthly courts of law," said Dorn. "There have been many battles out here. Wars that we paid for with our blood."

"Thousands?" Elverda repeated. "I knew that there had been occasional fights out here—but wars? I don't think anyone on Earth knows it's been so brutal."

"Men like Sterling know. They start the wars, and people like me fight them. Exiles, never allowed to return to Earth again once we take the mercenary's pay."

"All those men—killed."

Dorn nodded. "And women. The artifact made me see that it was my duty to find each of those forgotten bodies and give each one a decent final rite. The artifact seemed to be telling me that this was the path of my atonement."

"Your salvation," she murmured.

"I see now, however, that I underestimated the situation."

"How?"

"Sterling. While I am out there searching for the bodies of the slain, he will have me killed."

"No! That's wrong!"

Dorn's deep voice was empty of regret. "It will be simple for him to send a team after me. In the depths of dark space, they will murder me. What I failed to do for myself, Sterling will do for me. He will be my final atonement."

"Never!" Elverda blazed with anger. "I will not permit it to happen."

"Your own life is in danger from him," Dorn said.

"What of it? I am an old woman, ready for death."

"Are you?"

"I was . . . until I saw the artifact."

"Now life is more precious to you, isn't it?"

"I don't want you to die," Elverda said. "You have atoned for your sins. You have borne enough pain."

He looked away, then started up the tunnel again.

"You are forgetting one important factor," Elverda called after him.

Dorn stopped, his back to her. She realized now that the clothes he wore had been his military uniform. He had torn all the insignias and pockets from it.

"The artifact. Who created it? And why?"

Turning back toward her, Dorn answered, "Alien visitors to our solar system created it, unknown ages ago. As to why—you tell me: Why does someone create a work of art?"

"Why would aliens create a work of art that affects human minds?"

Dorn's human eye blinked. He rocked a step backward.

"How could they create an artifact that is a mirror to our

souls?" Elverda asked, stepping toward him. "They must have known something about us. They must have been here when there were human beings existing on Earth."

Dorn regarded her silently.

"They may have been here much more recently than you think," Elverda went on, coming closer to him. "They may have placed this artifact here to *communicate* with us."

"Communicate?"

"Perhaps it is a very subtle, very powerful communications device."

"Not an artwork at all."

"Oh yes, of course it's an artwork. All works of art are communications devices, for those who possess the soul to understand."

Dorn seemed to ponder this for long moments. Elverda watched his solemn face, searching for some human expression.

Finally he said, "That does not change my mission, even if it is true."

"Yes it does," Elverda said, eager to save him. "Your mission is to preserve and protect this artifact against Sterling and anyone else who would try to destroy it—or pervert it to his own use."

"The dead call to me," Dorn said solemnly. "I hear them in my dreams now."

"But why be alone in your mission? Let others help you. There must be other mercenaries who feel as you do."

"Perhaps," he said softly.

"Your true mission is much greater than you think," Elverda said, trembling with new understanding. "You have the power to end the wars that have destroyed your comrades, that have almost destroyed your soul."

"End the corporate wars?"

"You will be the priest of this shrine, this sepulcher. I will return to Earth and tell everyone about these wars."

"Sterling and others will have you killed."

"I am a famous artist, they dare not touch me." Then she laughed. "And I am too old to care if they do."

"The scientists—do you think they may actually learn how to communicate with the aliens?"

"Someday," Elverda said. "When our souls are pure enough to stand the shock of their presence."

The human side of Dorn's face smiled at her. He extended his arm and she took it in her own, realizing that she had found her own salvation. Like two kindred souls, like comrades who had shared the sight of death, like mother and son they walked up the tunnel toward the waiting race of humanity.

Background: Practice

Designing the Ringworld was the fun part. The difficult part would be describing it without losing the reader!
—Larry Niven

Larry Niven's novel *Ringworld* is a modern classic of science fiction. It is set on an artificial world built by alien engineers in the form of a gigantic ring around their star, a ring whose size is roughly equal to the size of the Earth's orbit around the Sun: a ring some three hundred million miles in circumference!

The novel is, in large part, an exploration of this stupendous artifact. Yet Niven masterfully tells a story about fascinating characters while he shows off this strange, engrossing world without losing the reader.

In a sense, the background of *Ringworld* was the novel's main attraction. Yet the background did not overwhelm Niven's story; it provided a magnificent stage on which the story is played out.

In "Sepulcher," the background is not merely the physical setting; there is a more important background suggested in the story, the social background. The story is set in a future time when human civilization has spread through much of the solar system. We are told that powerful corporations have built bases on the moons of Mars, on the asteroids that orbit between Mars and Jupiter, and even as far from Earth as Titan, the major moon of Saturn.

The story draws a picture of vast corporate wars in the depths of space, of whole giant space habitats destroyed in these wars, killing thousands of men, women and children. And there are "little guys" roaming through the solar system, too, such as the family of prospectors that discovers the alien artifact.

All of this happens off-stage, however. It is merely suggested. Only a few lines are devoted to this all-important background. But those few lines are enough to give the reader a sense of the world in which the story happens, the world in which the three characters live.

In "Fifteen Miles" (chapter four) the harsh lunar background served mainly two dramatic purposes: (1) to provide an isolated, forbidding setting for the physical ordeal that the protagonist had to go through; and (2) to provide an appropriate symbolic setting to mirror the protagonist's inner turmoil.

Thus the moon of "Fifteen Miles" was physically like the purgatory of Dante's *Divine Comedy*. Not that Kinsman faced punishing flames and devils. But the terraced inner walls of the crater Alphonsus form a natural analogy for the tiers of Dante's purgatory. In fact, hell itself was arranged in different levels by Dante, so it was necessary to have the priest tell Kinsman, at the end, that they were not in hell — which is eternal damnation — but in purgatory, which can be escaped after suffering purifying pain.

So the unnamed asteroid of "Sepulcher" also formed a specific physical background, a setting removed from the ordinary world, a cold, dead chunk of rock with a secret buried in its heart: the alien artifact.

It was not necessary to explain that human technology had reached a point where spacecraft routinely plied the asteroid belt looking for good chunks of metallic ores. Neither was it necessary to go into any detail whatever about how human engineers could build comfortable living quarters inside an asteroid. All I had to do was show the characters in action, and these background details came along with them, with hardly half a paragraph spent on them.

But look at the physical details I did put into the story: the special feeling of a low-gravity environment; colors, textures, tones of voice and other sensory clues to help you feel that you are there, experiencing what the characters of the story are going through. Light is especially important. I used it both to bring out various facets of the characters and in symbolic ways.

One of the symbolic ways I used light was in describing the character Dorn. He is seen entirely through the eyes of Elverda Apacheta, an artist who is at first repelled by the fact that Dorn is partly machine, a cybernetic organism, a cyborg. Despite herself, though, Elverda's artistic eyes begin to appreciate the grace and beauty of this man who is half human, half metal. And as she begins to soften toward him, the reader begins to learn more about Dorn's personal background.

CREATING "SEPULCHER"

Now for some words on the genesis of the story, the background of the creative process that led to "Sepulcher."

Most of my stories begin in my mind with a concept of the major character, or an intriguing situation that pops into my head and demands to be written about. "Sepulcher" was different. It began with an idea. For years I had a tiny scrap of paper tucked in my ideas file. It read, "Perfect artwork. Everyone sees themselves in it."

The idea intrigued me, but the reason that scrap of paper stayed in my file was that I knew the idea might be the background for a good story but was not sufficient for a story by itself. A good story needs believable characters in conflict.

As I mulled over the basic idea, I reasoned that the story would need several characters, so that the reader can see how this work of art affects different people. I began to see that the artwork would have to be an alien artifact. If a human being could create a work of art so powerful that everyone who sees it experiences a soul-shattering self-revelation, then the story would have to be about the artist and the power she gains over the rest of humankind.

That might make a terrific novel some day. But I was more interested in a short story about the work of art itself—and several people who are deeply, fundamentally changed by it. Thus I had actually created the basic background of the story before anything else.

I settled on three characters: a former soldier who had become a kind of holy man; a hard-driving man of vast wealth; and an artist who is near the end of her life. Each of them undergoes a transformation when they see the alien artwork.

Again, notice that much of the action takes place offstage. The mercenary soldier Dorik Harbin has already been transformed into the priest Dorn when the story begins. The billionaire's experience with the artifact is offstage. We see only the artist and her moment of truth as she sees the artwork and is transformed by it.

In the final analysis, "Sepulcher" is a story that deals with the *purpose* of art. Why do we create works of art? Why do painters paint their pictures and writers write their stories? Beneath all the other facets of "Sepulcher," that is the fundamental idea that we examine.

And that is the most important part of the background to good stories. Almost every story has a philosophical point to make. That may sound pretentious, but the simple truth is that all story-telling is based on getting across some truth that is culturally valid. Homer was trying to set a standard of conduct among his semi-barbaric listeners. The most vapid sitcom on commercial television reinforces the social norms of middle America.

Everything in a story's background should be shaped for the purpose of making the point that the author is striving for, and it is difficult for me to see any item of background information that could be removed without damaging the story's impact.

You might try that as an exercise: Reread the story and see if there are any parts of the background that can be removed without destroying the story's understandability and credibility. Try the same exercise with several other stories, including some of your own. You will be surprised at how much you can remove without hurting most stories. And perhaps you will be equally surprised at how much you must leave in.

Remember the old newspaperman's rule of thumb: "When in doubt, throw it out." Every part of the story's background must work to enhance the story. If it doesn't, get rid of it. Learn to be ruthless with your own prose. Often the scenes you like best will have to be cut out of the story. Do not let that worry you. The result will be a tighter, cleaner story. And if the scene is really all that good, it will start another story cooking in your mind.

REVIEW OF THE BACKGROUND CHECKLIST

Let us briefly examine this story, then, in the light of the checklist from chapter six.

1. **Make every background detail work.** There is not a detail in this story that does not help advance the mood or the character development or the plot. For example, we see at first that Dorn's

clothing is tattered, although his soldier's boots are highly polished. Later we learn that his clothing is his soldier's uniform, from which he has torn all the insignia and pockets: a physical representation of Dorn's soul-shaking decision to become a priest. He has torn away his military insignia because he has renounced soldiering. He has torn away the pockets because, as a self-styled priest, he has renounced all wealth.

Many of the details about Elverda show that she regards her life as over; she is an old woman, no longer capable of doing creative work, waiting for inevitable death. Perhaps longing for death to relieve her of her sense of failure. She feels cold. Is that because she is dying or because she misses the warmth of human family and friendships? But once she is changed by the alien artifact, once she realizes the enormity of what Dorn is telling her, she feels cold no longer. She has a reason to continue living. She has found a friend, a companion, perhaps the son she never bore.

Look for the other details in the story and see how each of them helps the story along.

2. Don't try to explain how the machinery works; just show what it does. There is not a word of explanation about any of the technological marvels in the story. Spacecraft and life-support systems and drawing computers and cyborgs—you see them in action without any description of how they work. Nor do I for an instant try to explain the alien artifact. It does what it does. Period. In fact, any attempt at explaining its mysterious marvels would weaken the story, distract from its impact.

In Stanley Kubrick's film *2001: A Space Odyssey*, the mysterious alien slab remains completely unexplained and stands as a powerful symbol of awe and mystery. Arthur C. Clarke's novel, on which the film was based, goes to some pains to explain what the slab is and how it works. And the story is thereby robbed of much of its mystery and majesty.

Save the explanations for academic papers or media interviews. As Nobel laureate chemist Peter DeBye often said, "Sometimes it is not so important to be right as to sound convincing."

3. Feel free to invent any new devices or scientific discoveries that you can imagine—providing they do not contradict what is known about science today. The far-flung interplanetary civilization that I postulate in "Sepulcher" depends on a lot of technological advances that have not yet been invented. But they undoubtedly will be. We currently know of no fundamental scientific reasons that would prohibit such a civilization.

The alien artifact is something else again. It is rather far-fetched, I grant, but no one can prove that such a device could never be made.

4. Be thoroughly familiar with the background of your story. I have been writing science fiction long enough and (more important) been involved in the world's real space programs long enough to be thoroughly familiar with the interplanetary setting of this story. The asteroid belt really exists. No one yet knows how many hundreds of thousands of chunks of rock and metal are floating out there in the belt, but many of them are literally small mountains of pure nickel-iron orbiting around the Sun. In 1991 NASA's *Galileo* spacecraft took the first close-up photograph of an asteroid, Gaspra, which is roughly the size of Manhattan island.

After nearly forty years of working among space technologists and scientists I have a decent knowledge from which to draw the background for "Sepulcher."

I was also quite familiar with the background of the story's central character, Elverda Apacheta. She had been a principle character in an earlier story of mine that bears the unlikely title, "A Can of Worms." It was in this tale that Elverda carved the mile-long asteroid she called *The Rememberer* and electronically painted *The Virgin of the Andes* across the ionospheric sky of North America.

5. Learn the basics of science. I am not a scientist, nor an engineer. I am a writer. But I fell in love with science the first time I went to a planetarium and began to see the majesty of the universe.

It is especially important to at least understand the fundamentals of science if you intend to write real science fiction stories. If you are more interested in the softer parts of SF, or in areas of writing that have nothing to do with science — learn science anyway! It is fun. It is the most human thing that human beings do: trying to understand the universe, from stars and galaxies down to microbes and the workings of our own minds. What could be more exciting? What could give you more material, and more understanding, for the stories you want to write?

6. Names are important. There are three named characters in "Sepulcher," and the names of all three of them were picked with great care.

Elverda Apacheta is a latter-day Incan princess. Her family name is the name of an Andean mountain tribe. In its native tongue, the name literally means "mountain people." Elverda is from the Latin for virgin; it is frequently given to Latin American girls born under the sign of Virgo.

Miles Sterling is the name of a very rich man. That ring of sterling silver is inescapable. So, perhaps, is the other meaning of sterling: excellence, solid worth, purity. It is obvious, once you see Sterling in action, that he is not excellent or pure. So, that meaning of his name also reverberates in the reader's mind as a reminder of what Miles Sterling is not.

Dorn is a name chosen almost entirely for its sound, although back in the 1940s a screen actor named Philip Dorn had the kind of rugged yet dour look to him that I imagine Dorn's human half-face to possess. His earlier name, Dorik Harbin, comes from a city in Manchuria — Harbin — that has known its share of destruction and misery under the heavy hand of Russian, Japanese and Chinese administration. Dorik just sounded right to me. It is a variant of a Polish name meaning, ironically, gift of god.

7. The background — and the story itself — must be internally consistent. I believe "Sepulcher" is internally consistent. The characters are in tune with the world in which they live; in fact, the reader only learns about that world through the characters' actions and words. An interplanetary civilization of ruthless capitalist corporations developing natural resources from the asteroids and other bodies in space, building and populating space habitats the size of modest cities, is engaged in cutthroat competition and even war. It seems not only internally consistent but almost inevitable, if the human race keeps expanding its numbers the way we are presently.

Which brings us to a final point: Every story must engross its readers so thoroughly that they fall into the world you have created with your words. The background of a story may be the exotic, magical world of *The Arabian Nights* or the hard-edged mean streets of Ed McBain's *87th Precinct* novels, but that background must help to create a kind of reality that possesses the reader from the first word of the tale to the last.

Chapter Nine

Conflict in Science Fiction

Conflict: Theory

The story . . . must be a conflict, and specifically, a conflict between the forces of good and evil within a single person.
—*Maxwell Anderson*

W hat is a story?

I have asked that question to hundreds of audiences ranging from students in writing classes to new acquaintances who immediately tell me that they want to be writers. I always ask anyone who expresses a desire to be a writer, "What is a story?"

I seldom get the answer I am looking for. Most people, even those who want to spend their lives writing stories, find it extraordinarily difficult to say exactly what a story is.

I have already given the answer, but I will repeat it here: A story is a narrative description of a character struggling to solve a problem. Nothing more than that. And nothing less.

There's an old Italian saying: "A meal without wine is like a day without sunshine." A story without conflict is like a meal without food. Conflict is what makes a story. How can you describe a character struggling to solve a problem without describing some form of conflict?

Without conflict, there is no story. You might have an interesting essay, or a lovely sketch of some scenes, or the setting and background for a story. But the story itself depends on conflict. Imagine what a drag *Romeo and Juliet* would be if the Montagues and Capulets were friendly and had no objections to a marriage between the two lovers. Or how boring *Moby Dick* would be if Ahab joined Greenpeace and gave up whale hunting.

SIMPLISTIC CONFLICT

The simplest form of conflict is the most obvious: action-packed fighting between two characters. This is the heart of the stereotypical western story—the good guy in the white hat shoots it out with the bad guy in the black hat. Or they fight it out with fists in the town saloon. This is called "horse opera," a justifiably derisive term when such physical action is the only kind of conflict in the story.

Science fiction stories have been written along the same lines, and such stories are called "space operas." They tend to be more grandiose and larger in scale than horse operas, because the science fiction writer has the whole universe of interstellar space to work with, instead of one dusty Western town. But the pattern is the same; physical action is the mainstay of the story. Instead of cattle rustlers in black hats we have an invasion of earth by horrid alien creatures. Instead of a battle with the Indians on the prairie we have an interstellar war. But the conflict is all physical, all good guys vs. bad guys.

Although space operas had virtually disappeared from science fiction writing by the 1960s, they are still a mainstay of Hollywood's sci-fi flicks, which usually draw their inspiration more from comic strips than from real science fiction published in books or magazines. In fact, sci-fi movies are about as closely related to science fiction as Popeye cartoons are to naval history.

The details of each space opera are somewhat different, of course, but the general pattern is almost invariably the same. There is a group of Good Guys. Usually they include at least one brilliant but eccentric scientist or other type of father figure, a beautiful young woman (often the scientist's beautiful daughter or some other relation) and one two-fisted hero. Then there are the Bad Guys. Sometimes they are invaders from outer space, but they can also be space pirates, interplanetary criminals, or a dictator and his henchmen. They usually have an evil scientist in their gang or, at the very least, the benefits of futuristic science, such as superweapons, hypnotic rays, invisible spaceships or whatnot.

The Good Guys fight the Bad Guys and win. Usually they have to come up with some dazzling new invention to win, and the hero often has to beat the chief villain in hand-to-hand combat. Whether it's *Star Wars* or *Alien* or *Outland*, every space opera offers little more in the way of conflict than physical shoot-'em-up.

The audience knows from the outset what the outcome will be. The thrill is in the chase and in the special effects.

There is no character development at all in most space operas, whether they are pulp-magazine tales of fifty years ago or this season's $50 million Hollywood extravaganzas. The hero, the villain, the other characters are completely unchanged by the action — except for a few bruises on the jut-jawed hero and the inevitable death of the slimy villain. There is no internal conflict in any of the characters. There is no real conflict between any of the characters, either, outside of the axiomatic Good Guy vs. Bad Guy fight. The entire cast of characters could go through exactly the same kind of story again in next month's issue of the pulp magazine or in the sequel to the movie.

Such stories seem ludicrously crude today, yet they still show up week after week in slushpiles all across the publishing industry. So let's get one thing straight right now: *Slam-bang action is not conflict.*

WHAT IS CONFLICT?

If you look up the word in a dictionary, you will find several definitions. The one that pertains to writers is: "clash or divergence of opinions, interests . . . a mental or moral struggle occasioned by incompatible desires, aims, etc."

A mental or moral struggle caused by incompatible desires and aims. That is the kind of conflict that makes stories vitally alive. Not merely the mindless, automatic violence of Good Guys vs. Bad Guys, but the clash of desires and aims that cannot coexist. Like the thunderstorms that boil up when two massive weather systems collide, the conflict in a story must well up from the inner beings of the major characters. This conflict can come in many forms; a fist in the face or a shoot-out is the least satisfying, because it takes the least thought to produce.

In a good story, the conflict exists at many different levels. It begins deep within the protagonist's psyche and wells up into conflicts between the protagonist and other characters and often — especially in science fiction — conflicts between the protagonist and the forces of nature or the strictures of society.

We saw in the chapters on character that the beginning of

every story is the emotional conflict within the protagonist's mind, such as *love* vs. *hate, fear* vs. *duty, loyalty* vs. *greed.*

In a short story, where the writer is cramped for space and time, the protagonist must begin the story with that inner emotional conflict already torturing him. Even in a novel, where you have much more flexibility and freedom, it is a good idea to have that central conflict already ablaze in the protagonist's heart. For now, let us stick with the problems you face when you must deal with conflict in a short story.

Whatever it was that caused the protagonist's inner conflict, it should have started before the first word of the story's opening. Sure, it may be possible to write an excellent short story in which you show the beginnings of the protagonist's agony. But as a rule, the story should be concerned with the *resolution* of the problem rather than its origins.

The short-story form is like a hundred-yard dash compared to a cross-country race. There is no time for pacing, strategy, getting a second wind. In a short dash you go flat out, and that's all. You write about the sequence of events (or the supreme, single event) that completely changes the protagonist's life, rather than telling the whole story of her existence. Novels are for telling life stories; short stories are for illuminating crucial incidents.

So the short story begins with the protagonist's inner conflict already boiling within. It is not necessary to blurt it out to the reader right at the outset, but the reader should quickly realize that here is a character with a problem.

Often it is the exterior manifestation of the protagonist's problem that is revealed first. In "The Second Kind of Loneliness," by George R. R. Martin, a young man has been tending a remote space station by himself for many months. The reader quickly sees that he is extremely lonely and awaiting the relief ship that will take him back to Earth. Only gradually does the reader come to realize that the man was extremely lonely even in the crowded cities of Earth. He was unable to make friends, to love anyone. He would be lonely no matter where he was.

In Robert Louis Stevenson's classic *Dr. Jekyll and Mr. Hyde,* the moral struggle between good and evil that rages within each human being is made physically real by the drug that transforms the humane Dr. Jekyll into the bestial Mr. Hyde. Stevenson is pointing out that there is a "Mr. Hyde" in all of us, which we struggle to suppress.

Most stories, though, revolve around a struggle between the protagonist and an opponent—an *antagonist*. In science fiction, of course, neither character need be actually human. But just as the protagonist must behave like a human being so that the reader will feel sympathy for him or her, the antagonist should also be human enough for the reader to at least understand what he, she or it is up to.

There is an important difference, incidentally, between an antagonist and a villain. It is very easy and very tempting, especially for a new writer, to create a villain who is mindlessly evil. That is, a villain who does bad things simply because the story needs bad things done.

That is why I prefer to use the word antagonist to describe the character who clashes against the protagonist. The antagonist does not realize that he is the villain of the story. He thinks he's the hero! Nobody, from Cain to Medea to Adolf Hitler, has ever really decided to take certain actions because they were the nasty, mean, villainous things to do. People firmly believe that everything they do—no matter how horrifying—is entirely justified, necessary, perhaps even saintly.

When you have a character who is doing rotten things merely for the sheer villainy of making problems for the hero, you have a weak story going. Villains, as well as heroes, must be motivated to act the way they do.

LEVELS OF CONFLICT

A strong story has many tiers of conflict. First is the inner struggle of the protagonist, *emotion* vs. *emotion*. Then this interior struggle is made exterior by focusing on an antagonist who attacks the protagonist precisely at her weakest point. The antagonist amplifies the protagonist's inner struggle, brings it out of her mind and into the outside world.

For example, think of the many layers of conflict in the tale of Robin Hood.

Interestingly, the Robin Hood stories were originally spoken, not written. They are folk tales. Over the many generations before the stories were gathered together in written form, the oral storytellers instinctively put plenty of conflict into the tales. They saw their audiences face to face and they knew what it took to keep them interested and wide-awake.

Robin's basic inner conflict is *obedience* vs. *justice*. He is an outstanding young nobleman, but his sense of justice forces him to become an outlaw. He must give up all that he holds dear and retreat into Sherwood Forest as a hunted man. His interior struggle is brought into the exterior world of action through his chief antagonist, the Sheriff of Nottingham. The sheriff represents law and order; Robin should be obedient to him. Yet, because the sheriff's idea of law and order conflicts with Robin's idea of justice and right, Robin and the sheriff are enemies.

So there are two levels of conflict going: Robin's inner struggle and his outer fight against the sheriff. To this are added many more minor conflicts and one overriding major conflict. The minor conflicts revolve around Robin's Merry Men, for the most part. Little John is not averse to knocking Robin into a stream the first time they meet. Friar Tuck and many of the other outlaws often have disagreements or fights with Robin—all in good fun, of course. But there is a steady simmering of conflict that has kept readers turning the pages of Robin's story for centuries.

The story is framed within a major conflict, the struggle between King Richard the Lion Heart and his scheming brother, Prince John. While comparatively few words in the story are devoted to this conflict, the struggle for the throne of England is actually the major force that motivates the story. We see only one small consequence of that royal struggle, the battle between Robin—a loyal follower of Richard—and the sheriff, who supports John.

Tier upon tier, the conflicts in a good story are multileveled. Of course, Robin Hood is not a short story. Yet it is possible to build many layers of conflict into short stories, as well.

Consider Vonda N. McIntyre's "Of Mist, and Grass, and Sand," which received the Nebula Award from the Science Fiction Writers of America in 1974.

The protagonist is a young woman, hardly more than a girl, who is a healer. Her name is Snake. Her healing instruments include three snakes, Mist, Grass and Sand, whom she uses as living biochemical laboratories, altering their venoms into various medicinal drugs.

Snake's inner conflict is *self* vs. *duty*. Being a healer is demanding, difficult and a lonely life. She must travel alone across the wilderness of her planet to answer the calls of the sick.

She is called to a small, backward village where a small boy is dying of a tumor. The parents of the boy and most of the villagers are terrified of her and her snakes. Yet, because they cannot allow the boy to die without trying to save him, they allow her to operate. To Snake's interior conflict we now add an outer conflict: the tension between her and the villagers. This outer conflict is also a matter of *self-interest* vs. *duty*: Snake could leave the village and its fearful, hostile people behind. But to do so would be to leave the child to die. She chooses to remain.

Treating the boy takes many, many hours. Snake begins to be attracted to one of the younger men of the village, who seems not quite as afraid of her as the others and even tries to help her in his clumsy way. More levels of conflict: Will Snake neglect her duty because of this love interest? Will the villagers start to accept her because this man accepts her, or will they turn against him because they hate and fear Snake?

In ignorance and fear, a villager kills one of the snakes, while the sick boy lies in a deathly coma. This brings out the conflict between Snake and the villagers even more sharply and adds another level of conflict, because Snake is responsible for her "instruments." Her superiors, who taught her how to heal, will blame her for the loss. Perhaps they will stop her from practicing the healing arts.

The boy recovers and the villagers are repentant. The young man asks Snake to stay with him. She must decide between love and duty. If she stays in the village and accepts the man's love, she will be turning her back on her life as a healer. If she goes back to her superiors, they may take that life away from her and she will lose everything, including the man's love.

Snake chooses to return to her superiors, risking their anger. She leaves the man behind. The conflicts are all resolved by this choice. It does not really matter if her superiors prevent her from practicing the healing arts again; her choice is made. She will face whatever fate has in store for her. She did not succumb to the temptation to stay in the village and give up her profession. She has chosen duty above self, and the reader feels that this is the morally correct choice. If she had chosen to stay in the village, she would have given up the part of herself that makes her herself. So, by choosing duty above self, she gains self-respect as well.

ALTERNATE ANTAGONISTS

In some science fiction stories, the antagonist is not a person at all. In "Flowers for Algernon," the classic short story by Daniel Keyes that he later expanded into a novel and turned into the movie *Charlie*, the antagonist is nature itself. Charlie's opponent is the universe, the blind inexorable workings of the laws of physics and chemistry.

Even though the antagonist may not be an individual character, the protagonist must have an opponent, and that opponent must work on the basic conflict within the soul of the protagonist. In "Fifteen Miles," the harsh environment of the moon can be thought of as Kinsman's antagonist, one that forced Kinsman to bring his inner turmoil into the open. There was much more to the story than the physical adventure problems of dragging an injured man through the wilderness to safety.

Conflict is what makes stories move. Stories that describe the author's idea of Utopia are unutterably dull; in the perfect society of Utopia, there are no conflicts. No conflict means no story. You can write a lovely travelogue about some beautiful world of the future. But if you want to make the reader keep turning pages, eager to find out what happens next, you must give the story as much conflict as you can stir up.

The writer's job is to be a troublemaker! Stir up as many levels of conflict and problems for your protagonist as you can. Let one set of problems grow out of another. And never, never, *never* solve a problem until you've raised at least two more. It is the unsolved problems that form the chain of promises that keeps the reader interested.

A CONFLICT CHECKLIST

1. A story is a narrative description of a character struggling to solve a problem. Nothing more, nothing less. *Struggle* means *conflict*.

2. In fiction, conflict almost always involves a mental or moral struggle between characters caused by incompatible desires and aims.

3. Physical action is not necessarily conflict.

4. The conflict in a story should be rooted in the mind of the protagonist; it is the protagonist's inner turmoil that drives the narrative.

5. The protagonist's inner struggle should be mirrored and amplified by an exterior conflict with an antagonist. The antagonist may be a character, nature, or the society in which the protagonist exists.

6. Eschew villains! The antagonist should believe that he is the hero of the tale.

7. Be a troublemaker! Create excruciating problems for your protagonist. And never solve one problem until you have raised at least two more—until the story's conclusion.

Chapter Ten

Conflict in Science Fiction

Crisis of the Month

A Complete Short Story

W hile I crumpled the paper note that someone had slipped into my jacket pocket, Jack Armstrong drummed his fingers on the immaculately gleaming expanse of the pseudomahogany conference table.

"Well," he said testily, "ladies and gentlemen, don't one of you have a possibility? An inkling? An idea?"

No one spoke. I left the wadded note in my pocket and placed both my hands conspicuously on the table top. Armstrong drummed away in abysmal silence. I guess once he had actually looked like The All-American Boy. Now, many facelifts and body remodelings later, he looked more like a moderately well-preserved dummy.

"Nothing at all, gentleman and ladies?" He always made certain to give each sex the first position 50 percent of the time. Affirmative action was a way of life with our Boss.

"Very well then. We will Delphi the problem."

That broke the silence. Everyone groaned.

"There's nothing else to be done," the Boss insisted. "We must have a crisis by Monday morning. It is now . . ." he glanced at the digital readout built into the table top, ". . . three-eighteen P.M. Friday. We will not leave this office until we have a crisis to offer."

We knew it wouldn't do a bit of good, but we groaned all over again.

The Crisis Command Center was the best-kept secret in the world. No government knew of our existence. Nor did the people, of course. In fact, in all the world's far-flung news media, only a select handful of the topmost executives knew of the CCC.

Those few, those precious few, that band of brothers and sisters—they were our customers. The reason for our being. They paid handsomely. And they protected the secret of our work even from their own news staffs.

Our job, our sacred duty, was to select the crisis that would be the focus of worldwide media attention for the coming month. Nothing more. Nothing less.

In the old days, when every network, newspaper, magazine, news service, or independent station picked out its own crises, things were always in a jumble. Sure, they would try to focus on one or two sure-fire headline-makers: a nuclear powerplant disaster or the fear of one, a new disease like AIDS or Chinese Rot, a war, terrorism, things like that.

The problem was, there were so many crises springing up all the time, so many threats and threats of threats, so much blood and fire and terror, that people stopped paying attention. The news scared the livers out of them. Sales of newspapers and magazines plunged toward zero. Audiences for news shows, even the revered network evening shows, likewise plummeted.

It was Jack Armstrong—a much younger, more handsome and vigorous All-American Boy—who came up with the idea of the Crisis Command Center. Like all great ideas, it was basically simple.

Pick one crisis each month and play it for all it's worth. Everywhere. In all the media. Keep it scary enough to keep people listening, but not so terrifying that they'll run away and hide.

And it worked! Worked to the point where the CCC (or Cee-Cubed, as some of our analysts styled it) was truly the command center for all the media of North America. And thereby, of course, the whole world.

But on this particular Friday afternoon, we were stumped. And I had that terrifying note crumpled in my pocket. A handwritten note, on paper, no less. Not an electronic communication, but a secret, private, dangerous seditious note, meant for me and me alone, surreptitiously slipped into my jacket pocket.

"Make big $$$," it scrawled. "Tell all to Feds."

I clasped my hands to keep them from trembling and wondered who, out of the fourteen men and women sitting around the table, had slipped that bomb to me.

Boss Jack had started the Delphi procedure by going down

the table, asking each of us board members in turn for the latest news in her or his area of expertise.

He started with the man sitting at his immediate right, Matt Dillon. That wasn't the name he had been born with, naturally; his original name had been Oliver Wolchinsky. But in our select little group, once you earn your spurs (no pun intended) you are entitled to a "power name," a name that shows you are a person of rank and consequence. Most power names were chosen, of course, from famous media characters.

Matt Dillon didn't look like the marshal of Dodge City. Or even the one-time teen screen idol. He was short, pudgy, bald, with bad skin and an irritable temper. He looked, actually, exactly as you would expect an Oliver Wolchinsky to look.

But when Jack Armstrong said, "We shall begin with you," he added, "Matthew."

Matt Dillon was the CCC expert on energy problems. He always got to his feet when he had something to say. This time he remained with his round rump resting resignedly on the caramel cushion of his chair.

"The outlook is bleak," said Matt Dillon. "Sales of the new space-manufactured solar cells are still climbing. Individual homes, apartment buildings, condos, factories—everybody's plastering their roofs with them and generating their own electricity. No pollution, no radiation, nothing for us to latch onto. They don't even make noise!"

"Ah," intoned our All-American Boy, "but they must be ruining business for electric utility companies. Why not a crisis there?" He gestured hypnotically, and put on an expression of Ratheresque somberness, intoning, "Tonight we will look at the plight of the electrical utilities, men and women who have been discarded in the stampede for cheap energy."

"Trampled," a voice from down the table suggested.

"Ah, yes. Instead of discarded. Thank you." Boss Jack was never one to discourage creative criticism.

But Marshal Matt mewed, "The electric utility companies are doing just fine; they invested in the solar cell development back in '95. They saw the handwriting in the sky."

A collective sigh of disappointment went around the table.

Not one to give up easily, our Mr. Armstrong suggested, "What about oil producers, then? The coal miners?"

"The last coal miner retired on full pension in '98," replied Matt dolefully. "The mines were fully automated by then. Nobody cares if robots are out of work; they just get reprogrammed and moved into another industry. Most of the coal robots are picking fruit in Florida now."

"But the Texas oil and gas. . . ."

Matt headed him off at the pass. "Petroleum prices are steady. They sell the stuff to plastics manufacturers, mostly. Natural gas is the world's major heating fuel. It's clean, abundant and cheap."

Gloom descended on our conference table.

It deepened as Boss Jack went from one of our experts to the next.

Terrorism had virtually vanished in the booming world economy.

Political scandals were depressingly rare: With computers replacing most bureaucrats there was less cheating going on in government, and far fewer leaks to the media.

The space program was so successful that no less than seven governments of space-faring nations — including our own dear Uncle Sam — had declared dividends for their citizens and a tax amnesty for the year.

Population growth was nicely leveling off. Inflation was minimal. Unemployment was a thing of the past, with an increasingly roboticized workforce encouraging humans to invest in robots, accept early retirement, and live off the productivity of their machines.

The closest thing to a crisis in that area was a street brawl in St. Petersburg between two retired Russian factory workers — aged thirty and thirty-two — who both wanted the very same robot. Potatoes that were much too small for our purposes.

There hadn't been a war since the International Peacekeeping Force had prevented Fiji from attacking Tonga, nearly twelve years ago.

Toxic wastes, in the few remote regions of the world where they still could be found, were being gobbled up by genetically altered bugs (dubbed Rifkins, for some obscure reason) that happily died once they had finished their chore and dissolved into harmless water, carbon dioxide and ammonia compounds. In some parts of the world the natives had started laundry and cleaning establishments on the sites of former toxic waste dumps.

I watched and listened in tightening terror as the fickle finger of fate made its way down the table toward me. I was low man on the board, the newest person there, sitting at the end of the table between pert Ms. Mary Richards (sex and family relations were her specialty) and dumpy old Alexis Carrington-Colby (nutrition and diets — it was she who had, three months earlier, come up with the blockbuster of the "mother's milk" crisis).

I hoped desperately that either Ms. Richards or Ms. Carrington-Colby would offer some shred of hope for the rest of the board to nibble on, because I knew I had nothing. Nothing except that damning, damaging note in my pocket. What if the Boss found out about it? Would he think I was a potential informer, a philandering fink to the Feds?

With deepening despair I listened to flinty-eyed Alexis offer apologies instead of ideas. It was Mary Richards' turn next, and my heart began fluttering unselfishly. I liked her, I was becoming quite enthusiastic about her, almost to the point of asking her romantic questions. I had never dated a sex specialist, or much of anyone, for that matter. Mary was special to me, and I wanted her to succeed.

She didn't. There was no crisis in sex or family relations.

"Mr. James," said the Boss, like a bell tolling for a funeral.

I wasn't entitled to a power name, since I had only recently been appointed to the board. My predecessor, Marcus Welby, had keeled over right at this conference table the previous month when he realized that there was no medical crisis in sight. His heart broke, literally. It had been his fourth one, but this time the rescue team was just a shade too late to pull him through again.

Thomas K. James is hardly a power name. But it was the one my parents had bestowed on me, and I was determined not to disgrace it. And in particular, not to let anyone know that someone in this conference room thought I was corruptible.

"Mr. James," asked a nearly weeping All-American Boy, "is there anything on the medical horizon — anything at all — that may be useful to us?"

It was clear that Boss Armstrong did not suspect me of incipient treason. Nor did he expect me to solve his problem. I did not fail him in that expectation.

"Nothing worth raising an eyebrow over, sir, I regret to say." Remarkably, my voice stayed firm and steady, despite the dervishes dancing in my stomach.

"There are no new diseases," I went on, "and the old ones are still in rapid retreat. Genetic technicians can correct every identifiable malady in the zygotes, and children are born healthy for life." I cast a disparaging glance at Mr. Cosby, our black environmentalist, and added, "Pollution-related diseases are so close to zero that most disease centers around the world no longer take statistics on them."

"Addiction!" he blurted, the idea apparently springing into his mind unexpectedly. "There must be a new drug on the horizon!"

The board members stirred in their chairs and looked hopeful. For a moment.

I burst their bubble. "Modern chemotherapy detoxifies the addict in about eleven minutes, as some of us know from first-hand experience." I made sure not to stare at Matt Dillon or Alexis Carrington-Colby, who had fought bouts with alcohol and chocolate, respectively. "And, I must unhappily report, cybernetic neural programming is mandatory in every civilized nation in the world; once an addictive personality manifests itself, it can be reprogrammed quickly and painlessly."

The gloom around the table deepened into true depression, tinged with fear.

Jack Armstrong glanced at the miniature display screen discreetly set into the tabletop before him, swiftly checking on his affirmative actions, then said, "Ladies and gentleman, the situation grows more desperate with each blink of the clock. I suggest we take a five-minute break for R and R (he meant relief and refreshment) and then come back with some *new ideas!*"

He fairly roared out the last two words, shocking us all.

I repaired to my office—little more than a cubicle, actually, but it had a door that could be shut. I closed it carefully and hauled the unnerving note out of my pocket. Smoothing it on my desk top, I read it again. It still said:

"Make big $$$. Tell all to Feds."

I wadded it again and with trembling hands tossed it into the disposal can. It flashed silently into healthful ions.

"Are you going to do it?"

I wheeled around to see Mary Richards leaning against my

door. She had entered my cubicle silently and closed the door without a sound. At least, no sound I had heard, so intent was I on that menacing message.

"Do what?" Lord, my voice cracked like Henry Aldrich.

Mary Richards (nee Stephanie Quaid) was a better physical proximation to her power name than any one of the board members, with the obvious exception of our revered Boss. She was the kind of female for whom the words cute, pert and vivacious were created. But beneath those skin-deep qualities she had the ruthless drive and calculated intelligence of a sainted Mike Wallace. Had to. Nobody without the same could make it to the CCC board. If that sounds self-congratulatory, so be it. A real Mary Richards, even a Lou Grant, would never get as far as the front door of the CCC.

"Tell all to the Feds," she replied sweetly.

The best thing I could think of was, "I don't know what you're talking about."

"The note you just ionized."

"What note?"

"The note I put in your pocket before the meeting started."

"You?" Until that moment I hadn't known I could hit high C.

Mary positively slinked across my cubicle and draped herself on my desk, showing plenty of leg through her slitted skirt. I gulped and slid my swivel chair into the corner.

"It's okay, there're no bugs operating in here. I cleared your office this morning."

I could feel my eyes popping. "Who are you?"

Her smile was all teeth. "I'm a spy, Tommy. A plant. A deep agent. I've been working for the Feds since I was a little girl, rescued from the slums of Chicago by the Rehabilitation Corps from what would have undoubtedly been a life of gang violence and prostitution."

"And they planted you here?"

"They planted me in Cable News when I was a fresh young thing just off the Rehab Farm. It's taken me eleven years to work my way up to the CCC. We always suspected some organization like this was manipulating the news, but we never had the proof. . . ."

"Manipulating!" I was shocked at the word. "We don't manipulate."

"Oh?" She seemed amused at my rightful ire. "Then what do you do?"

"We select. We focus. We manage the news for the benefit of the public."

"In my book, Tommy old pal, that is manipulation. And it's illegal."

"It's . . . out of the ordinary channels," I granted.

Mary shook her pretty chestnut-brown tresses. "It's a violation of FCC regulations, it makes a mockery of the antitrust laws, to say nothing of the SEC, OSHA, ICC, WARK, and a half a dozen other regulatory agencies."

"So you're going to blow the whistle on us."

She straightened up and sat on the edge of my desk. "I can't do that, Tommy. I'm a government agent. An agent provocateur, I'm sure Mr. Armstrong's lawyers will call me."

"Then, what. . . ."

"You can blow the whistle," she said smilingly. "You're a faithful employee. Your testimony would stand up in court."

"Destroy," I spread my arms in righteous indignation, "all this?"

"It's illegal as hell, Tom," said Mary. "Besides, the rewards for being a good citizen can be very great. Lifetime pension. Twice what you're making here. Uncle Sam is very generous, you know. We'll fix you up with a new identity. We'll move you to wherever you want to live: Samoa, Santa Barbara, St. Thomas even Schenectady. You could live like a retired financier."

I had to admit, "That is . . . generous."

"And," she added, shyly lowering her eyes, "of course I'll have to retire, too, once the publicity of the trial blows my cover. I won't have the same kind of super pension that you'll get, but maybe. . . ."

My throat went dry.

Before I could respond, though, the air-raid siren went off, signaling that the meeting was reconvening.

I got up from my chair, but Mary stepped between me and the door.

"What's your answer, Thomas?" she asked, resting her lovely hands on my lapels.

"I . . ." gulping for air, ". . . don't know."

She kissed me lightly on the lips. "Think it over, Thomas dear. Think hard."

It wasn't my thoughts that were hardening. She left me standing in the cubicle, alone except for my swirling thoughts spinning through my head like a tornado. I could hear the roaring in my ears. Or was that simply high blood pressure?

The siren howled again, and I bolted to the conference room and took my seat at the end of the table. Mary smiled at me and patted my knee, under the table.

"Very well," said Jack Armstrong, checking his display screen, "gentleman and ladies. I have come to the conclusion that if we cannot find a crisis anywhere in the news," and he glared at us, as if he didn't believe there wasn't a crisis out there somewhere, probably right under our noses, "then we must manufacture a crisis."

I had expected that. So had most of the other board members, I could see. What went around the table was not surprise but resignation.

Cosby shook his head wearily, "We did that last month, and it was a real dud. The Anguish of Kindergarten. Audience response was a negative four-point-four. Negative!"

"Then we've got to be more creative!" snapped The All-American Boy.

I glanced at Mary. She was looking at me, smiling her sunniest smile, the one that could allegedly turn the world on. And the answer to the whole problem came to me with that blinding flash that marks true inspiration and minor epileptic fits.

This wasn't epilepsy. I jumped to my feet. "Mr. Armstrong! Fellow board members!"

"What is it, Mr. James?" Boss Jack replied, a hopeful glimmer in his eyes.

The words almost froze in my throat. I looked down at Mary, still turning out megawatts of smile at me, and nearly choked because my heart had jumped into my mouth.

But only figuratively. "Ladies and gentlemen," (I had kept track, too), "there is a spy among us from the Federal Regulatory Commissions."

A hideous gasp arose, as if they had heard the tinkling bell of a leper.

"This is no time for levity, Mr. James," snapped the Boss.

"On the other hand, if this is an attempt at shock therapy to stir the creative juices. . . ."

"It's real!" I insisted. Pointing at the smileless Mary Richards, I said, "This woman is a plant from the Feds. She solicited my cooperation. She tried to bribe me to blow the whistle on the CCC!"

They stared. They snarled. They hissed at Mary. She rose coolly from her chair, made a little bow, blew me a kiss, and left the conference room.

Armstrong was already on the intercom phone. "Have security detain her and get our legal staff to interrogate her. Do it now!"

Then the Boss got to his feet, way down there at the other end of the table, and fixed me with his steeliest gaze. He said not a word, but clapped his hands together, once, twice. . . .

And the entire board stood up for me and applauded. I felt myself blushing, but it felt good. Warming. My first real moment in the sun.

The moment ended too soon. We all sat down and the gloom began to gray over my sunshine once more.

"It's too bad, Mr. James, that you didn't find a solution to our problem rather than a pretty government mole."

"Ah, but sir," I replied, savoring the opportunity for *le mot just*, "I have done exactly that."

"What?"

"You mean . . . ?"

"Are you saying that you've done it?"

I rose once more, without even glancing at the empty chair at my left.

"I have a crisis, sir." I announced quietly, humbly.

Not a word from any of them. They all leaned forward, expectantly, hopefully, yearningly.

"The very fact that we—the leading experts in the field—can find no crisis is in itself a crisis," I told them.

They sighed, as if a great work of art had suddenly been unveiled.

"Think of the crisis management teams all around the world who are idle! Think of the psychologists and the therapists who stand ready to help their fellow man and woman, yet have nothing to do! Think of the vast teams of news reporters, camera persons, editors, producers, publishers, even golfers, the whole vast panoply of men and women who have dedicated their lives to bringing the latest crisis into the homes of every human being on this planet—with nothing more to do than report on sports and weather!"

They leaped to their feet and converged on me. They raised me to their shoulders and joyously carried me around the table, shouting praises.

Deliriously happy, I thought to myself, I won't be at the foot of the table anymore. I'll move up. One day, I'll be at the head of the table, where The All-American Boy is now. He's getting old, burnt out. I'll get there. I'll get there!

And I knew what my power name would be. I'd known it from the start, when I'd first been made the lowliest member of the board. I'd been saving it, waiting until the proper moment to make the change.

My power name would be different, daring. A name that bespoke true power, the ability to command, the vision to see far into the future. And it wouldn't even require changing my real name that much. I savored the idea and rolled my power name through my mind again as they carried me around the table. Yes, it would work. It was right.

I would no longer be Thomas K. James. With the slightest, tiniest bit of manipulation my true self would stand revealed: James T. Kirk.

I was on my way.

Chapter Eleven

Conflict in Science Fiction

Conflict: Practice

You gain strength, courage and confidence by every experience in which you really stop to look fear in the face . . . You must do the thing which you think you cannot do.

—Eleanor Roosevelt

Mrs. Roosevelt was not giving advice to writers when she wrote those words, but better advice would be hard to find. As a writer, you must do the thing which you think you cannot do; push yourself farther, stretch your writerly muscles, reach for impossible dreams. Also, you must push your characters to do what they think they cannot do; give them conflicts that they cannot possibly resolve. Then get them to resolve them.

Even a lighthearted story such as "Crisis of the Month" can have plenty of conflict in it. In fact, no matter what the mood of a story, if it does not crackle with conflict there is no interest, no point, no story.

Conflict was at the very core of my thoughts when I first began to write "Crisis of the Month." The story began when my wife complained one evening about the hysterical manner in which the news media report on the day's events. Veteran newscaster Linda Ellerbee calls the technique "anxiety news." Back in journalism school (so long ago that spelling was considered important) I was taught that "good news is no news." Today's media take this advice to extremes: No matter what the story, there is a down side to it that can be emphasized—and usually is.

So when my darling and very perceptive wife complained about the utterly negative way in which the media presented the day's news, I quipped, "I can see the day when science finally finds out how to make people immortal. The media will do stories about the sad plight of the funeral directors."

My wife is also one of the top literary agents in the business. She immediately suggested, "Why don't you write a story about that?"

Thus the origin of "Crisis of the Month."

Notice that the story has nothing to do with achieving immortality or with funeral directors. But that is where the idea originally sprang from. And the originating idea was rich in several forms of conflict: various characters in conflict with one another, the government in conflict with the media, the very idea of a Crisis Command Center that manages the news in conflict with our inherent concept of freedom of the press.

The background to the story is suggested, not shown. "Crisis of the Month" takes place in a lovely, peaceful, healthy world; so lovely and peaceful and healthy, in fact, that its very desirable attributes provide a level of conflict. How can a Crisis Command Center do its job if there are no crises? All of this is shown through the dialogue among the characters. The setting of the story is confined to the offices of the CCC.

Two forms of conflict hit the reader on the very first page. The protagonist, Thomas K. James, is worried about a note he has crumpled up and stuffed into his pocket, and the CCC board chairman, Jack Armstrong, is distinctly unhappy with his crew. To find out why, the reader must go deeper into the story.

Remember that the basis of conflict lies in the protagonist's inner struggle of one emotion battling against another. With Thomas K. James, that inner struggle is his desire to succeed and become a full-fledged member of the CCC board versus his fear that he does not have what it takes to succeed.

Ambition vs. *self-doubt.*

Enter Mary Richards, who brings that inner turmoil out into the open in two different ways: One, Tom James is powerfully attracted to Mary Richards; romance is in the air. Two, it turns out that Mary is a government agent who wants him to be a witness against the CCC. This creates another level of conflict: If Tom goes along with Mary, he will sabotage the CCC and ruin his own career; if he refuses to work against the CCC, he will certainly lose Mary.

Loyalty vs. *love.*

Through all this there is still another level of conflict confronting the reader: Is it right to have a Crisis Command Center? Should these people be allowed to manage the news, month after month? Should Tom sell out to the Feds? Wouldn't that be the right thing to do?

"Crisis of the Month" is also a variation of what I call the "jailbreak" plot. Chances are that you think what the CCC is doing is wrong, and therefore Tom is wrong to be with them. The protagonist is doing something that you feel is morally wrong, like a convict attempting to break out of jail. Yet because the protagonist is sympathetically drawn, the reader wants the protagonist to succeed, even though the protagonist may be doing "wrong" in the eyes of society.

In its original form, the jailbreak story put the reader on the horns of a moral dilemma. You want the protagonist to succeed, yet you know that the protagonist's success is socially wrong. The prisoner-of-war variation of the jailbreak story removes this moral ambiguity—as long as it is *our* POWs trying to break out of the enemy's camp.

In "Crisis of the Month" all of this is lighthearted, of course. Yet within the context of the story it is these various levels of conflict that keep the reader turning pages, anxious to find out what happens next.

At the story's climax, Tom opts to save the CCC despite the fact that it will cost him Mary's love (assuming that she truly loved him, which is doubtful). Once he makes that tough decision, he also comes up with the solution to the CCC's problem and receives the reward he wanted all along: recognition by the other board members and the right to chose his own "power name."

Despite the playful tone of the story, what Tom does seems somehow wrong in the reader's eyes. He has thrown away his chance for True Love in order to further the nefarious work of an organization that manages the news, which strikes a jarring chord among those of us who would like to believe the news media are scrupulously fair and independent. In the very end Tom makes a morally reprehensible choice and is rewarded with all the wealth and approval that the CCC can bestow. And, chances are, the reader wanted Tom to succeed! So the tale ends on a note of moral conflict within the reader's mind.

We have come a long way from the simple fistfight or shoot-out, in our examination of conflict. Certainly there is nothing wrong with physical action as a source of conflict in a story. Homer had plenty of battles in the *Iliad*, for example. But there are other, better choices available. In science fiction, as we have seen, the path is wide open to set the protagonist in struggle against the forces of nature or the bounds of a stifling society.

Yet, whatever kinds of conflict you put into your stories—whether it is a martial arts fight or a military rebellion against a dictatorship—the fundamental, underlying conflict must always be the struggle going on within the mind of the protagonist. Out of his interior conflict stem all the other conflicts of the story. If the protagonist has no inner turmoil, the story is quite literally gutless, and all the slam-bang action in the world will be nothing more than mindless, unnecessary and ultimately boring violence.

REVIEW OF THE CONFLICT CHECKLIST

This time, let us use the checklist as the basis for a quiz.

1. A story is a narrative description of a character struggling to solve a problem. Nothing more; nothing less. *Struggle* means *conflict.* Who is the protagonist in "Crisis of the Month?" What is the protagonist's problem? As a mental exercise, think of rewriting the story from another character's point of view. Which character would you pick? What would be the protagonist's problem?

2. In fiction, conflict almost always involves a mental or moral struggle between characters caused by incompatible desires and aims. What are the desires and aims of the protagonist? Whose desires and aims conflict with them?

3. Physical action is not necessarily conflict. Is there any physical action in the story? If not, did you find the story static or dull?

4. The conflict in a story should be rooted in the mind of the protagonist; it is the protagonist's inner turmoil that drives the narrative. Earlier in the chapter I gave the protagonist's basic inner conflict in the form of an equation of *emotion* vs. *emotion.* What were the two emotions? Could you write a similar equation for Mary Richards or Jack Armstrong?

5. The protagonist's inner struggle should be mirrored and amplified by an exterior conflict with an antagonist. The antago-

nist may be a character, nature, or the society in which the protagonist exists. Who is the antagonist in this story? Jack Armstrong? Mary Richards? The government? The society as a whole?

6. Eschew villains! The antagonist should believe that he is the hero of the tale. Could you rewrite this story with Mary Richards as the protagonist? Make a one-page outline of that.

7. Be a troublemaker! Create excruciating problems for your protagonist. And never solve one problem until you have raised at least two more — until the story's conclusion. Go through the story and count the problems that the protagonist faces. Note when each problem is solved. And note that the resolution of the story solves the basic problem shown at the story's beginning — even though you may not like the morality of the solution!

Chapter Twelve

Plot in Science Fiction

Plot: Theory

Draw your chair up close to the edge of the precipice and I'll tell you a story.

    —F. Scott Fitzgerald

Gordon R. Dickson is not only a fine writer, but also one of the best story "doctors" I know. Writers take their problem stories to Gordy for advice.

He was once asked, "What makes a story tick?" His answer: "The time bomb that's set to explode on the last page."

Every story is a race against time. Something is going to happen and, whether it is good or bad, the characters and events of the story are set up to get to the time and place where that something is going to come off. Perhaps it is as simple as pointing out that the emperor's invisible new clothes are actually nonexistent. Or as complex as the super nuclear device called the doomsday machine, which literally destroys the world in Stanley Kubrick's motion picture *Dr. Strangelove*.

Even in a long and complex novel, there is still that time bomb ticking away, page after page. Its beat may be muffled or slow, but it is there, chapter after chapter. In Frank Herbert's *Dune*, it was that ultimate moment when rain first begins to fall on the desert world of Arakis. In Tom Clancy's *The Hunt for Red October*, it was the question of whether or not the Soviet submarine captain would succeed in his effort to escape his pursuers.

In a short story the time bomb must tick loudly on every page, from the opening paragraph to the end of the tale. "The game's afoot," as Sherlock Holmes says, and that race against time is especially sharp in a short story, where you must engage your reader immediately and start those pages turning.

In some stories, the time bomb can be more subtle and more complex. In Isaac Asimov's "Nightfall," it was the threat of the destruction of civilization on a planet that is always lit by its multiple suns, except for one brief night every thousand years. In Arthur C. Clarke's "The Nine Billion Names of God," a sect of Tibetan lamas are convinced that God has nine billion names, and the world will end once humankind has written them all down. They have been laboriously doing the job by hand for centuries, but now they buy a computer to finish the task within a few days. I will never forget the shiver that went up my spine when the computer finally printed out the nine billionth name.

But simple or complex, subtle or bluntly obvious, the time bomb represents a threat, and its ticking should be loud and clear on the very first page of the story. The writer must promise the reader that the story's protagonist is going to face an incredibly difficult problem, dangers that are overwhelming, enemies that are unbeatable, conflicts that will tear her apart.

In most stories the time bomb has several different aspects; the explosion promised at the end of the tale can happen at many different levels — as many, in fact, as the various levels of conflict built into the story. In "Fifteen Miles," the ticking of the time bomb is a countdown that will end with either the success or failure of Kinsman's efforts to save the priest, and the success or failure of his efforts to keep his secret to himself. Note that the protagonist cannot succeed in both efforts. The two conflicts also conflict with each other, placing the protagonist on the horns of an impossible dilemma.

Think about "Sepulcher" and "Crisis of the Month" with an eye to understanding what the time bombs are in those stories and on how many different levels they might explode.

SETTING THE PLOT TICKING

The essence of creating a strong, exciting plot lies in building a powerful time bomb and making certain that the reader can hear its ticking from the very first page — even the first paragraph — of the story. The three aspects of fiction writing that we have already discussed — character, background and conflict — must be brought into focus by the plot. The protagonist must have a problem that she must solve. To solve this problem the protagonist will come into conflict with other characters and/or the environment in which the story is set. The background of the story must contribute to the protagonist's struggle.

Some writers begin planning a story by constructing a plot, then putting in characters, background and conflict as necessary. For example, they start with a basic idea, such as, What would happen if the least intelligent people of the world had larger and larger families, while the most intelligent had fewer and fewer children? The answer turned into Cyril M. Kornbluth's classic, "The Marching Morons," one of the best novelettes ever written in the science fiction genre. I may be entirely wrong, but it seems to me that Kornbluth got the basic idea first, worked out a plot to suit the idea, and then peopled the story with the characters, background and conflicts that it needed.

On the other hand, it is possible to get the germ of a story idea from any point of the compass and build the story from that starting place. Asimov's "Nightfall" began with the background of a planet where night comes only once each thousand years. "Sepulcher" began with the idea of a work of art so perfectly executed that all who see it see something specific to their own life. "Crisis of the Month" began as a grumble about the way the news media seem constantly to seek out anxiety-producing stories.

Many science fiction short stories begin with an idea about a gimmick: an invention, a problem, an exotic new background. Then the writer works out the characters and plot to showcase the idea. Thus we get a steady succession of what are called "gimmick stories": brilliant protagonist runs into impossible problem and solves it with brilliant invention or deduction or improvisation or whatnot. Gimmick stories can be fun to read, but they seldom leave a lasting impression. They are like eating popcorn: It tastes good at the time, but there's very little lasting value.

There have been so many gimmick stories in science fiction that both readers and editors have become very critical of them. Unless the story has a truly surprising twist to it, the science fiction audience will probably figure out the ending well ahead of time, and thus the story's suspense value is ruined.

The stories that last, the stories that really stay in the readers' minds, are usually stories that have a strong interplay between a very sympathetically drawn protagonist and a powerful, overwhelming problem. The writer's task is to make the reader care about the protagonist. Tie him to a chair and put a bomb at his feet; then make certain that the bomb's clock ticks loudly.

GIVING STRENGTH TO YOUR PLOTS

For me, as a writer, the best way to build a good plot is to begin with a strong, sympathetic protagonist and put him into action against a similarly strong antagonist.

Strong, in this context, does not necessarily mean the jutting jaw, steely eyes and bulging muscles of the typical old-time pulp magazine hero. In a novelette called "The Dueling Machine" (which I later expanded into a novel), my protagonist was a gangling, bumbling young man who could barely walk across a room without getting into trouble. His antagonist was an equally young man who had athletic and martial arts skills. But the protagonist had strengths that the antagonist lacked, chiefly sincerity, honesty, and a dogged, stubborn kind of heroism that could take a lot of punishment without admitting defeat.

As Kipling pointed out in his *Ballad of East and West*:

> But there is neither East nor West,
> Border, nor Breed, nor Birth,
> When two strong men stand face to face, tho'
> they come from the ends of the earth.

If you can place two strong characters "face to face," in conflict with each other, they will build the plot of the story for you. All you need to do is give them something to struggle over and a background in which to carry on the conflict. It might be a chess tournament, as in Fritz Leiber's "The Sixty-Four Square Madhouse"; or a struggle between a lone individual and a lock-step conformist society, as in Harlan Ellison's " 'Repent, Harlequin!' Said the Ticktockman"; or the brutality of war, as in Joe Haldeman's novel, *The Forever War*.

In a short story there is very little room or time for a deeply probing psychological analysis of the characters, or a gradual building up of plot and conflict. Particularly in a science fiction short story, where so much effort must be spent on making the background understandable and believable, the writer must open the story with that noisy time bomb.

Most new writers do not understand that, although once in a while a newcomer hits that particular nail squarely. Scott W. Schumack accomplished it quite nicely in his first published work, "Persephone and Hades." Here are the opening lines of his story:

> This is the way legends are born.
> Twenty-three hours out of twenty-four Carver hunted her. He crept silently through the labyrinthine corridors and artificial caverns of the Necropolis, armed, wary of ambush, and above all, hating her.

In those few lines, the writer has established the protagonist, the antagonist, the background setting and a conflict. More than that. He has dangled what is called the "narrative hook" in front of the reader's eyes, and the reader bites on it immediately. We want to know more: who, why, where, when, how? The time bomb is ticking loud and clear in those first two paragraphs. We know it is going to explode, and we want to find out what is happening.

NURTURING PLOT SURPRISES

Every plot needs a few surprising twists and turns, of course. But even here it is best to let the characters themselves surprise you, the writer. If you have developed a set of interesting characters, people who are alive in your mind, you will find that they start to do surprising things as you write their story. They will take over their own destinies and stubbornly resist your efforts to bend them to a preconceived plot. The antagonist that you wanted to put in jail will squeeze out of your trap. The protagonist whom you thought would go off in one direction will suddenly decide to do something completely different.

Let them! As long as the characters are working on the conflict-problem that they started the story with, let them do things their own way. But when they drop the original problem and begin working on something new, then you have a serious flaw in the story. Either the problem you started to write about is not working well, or you've gotten off the track of the story completely. Then you must decide whether to scrap what you have written and return to the original story line or scrap the original idea and let the characters go their own way.

Next to the opening of a short story, the ending is the most critical section. The ending must at the same time surprise your readers and convince them of its inevitable logic. A good short story ends like a good joke: with a snap that surprises and delights. But the ending must also be consistent with the main body of the story. You cannot have the titanically powerful villain, who has the hero at his mercy, suddenly drop dead of a gratuitous heart attack. Neither can you have the heroine abruptly decide that the world is too much for her and commit suicide.

Many new writers work very hard to pull a surprise ending out of their stories. Surprises are fine, but only when they are consistent with the rest of the story. I think that O. Henry has ruined many a promising young writer, because they read his "twist" endings in school and spend the rest of their writing careers trying to emulate him. Their careers are usually short, unless they outgrow the temptation to write surprise endings.

Surprises are fine at the end of a story, but surprise endings are dangerous. To explain: O. Henry's stories were written around the final punch line. Take away the ending and there is no real story. O. Henry did it masterfully, but it is essentially a gimmick, a trick that has very limited uses. New writers should plot their stories around main characters and their conflicts, not around a trick ending. Otherwise, they produce an essentially dull, uninspired piece of work that depends entirely on the whopper at the very end.

BUILDING STORY FLOW

Some writers like to make fairly detailed outlines of their stories, so that they know almost exactly what is going to happen, scene by scene. This makes some sense for longer works such as novels, where the plot can get quite complicated. We will discuss outlining for novels in chapter fifteen. But for the short story, outlines can sometimes be a hindrance rather than a help.

If the story is to flow out of the conflict between the two major characters (or the protagonist's conflict with the environment), a detailed outline might just strangle the characters' freedom of action. If the writer forces the characters to move from scene to scene and speak the dialogue necessary for each scene exactly as outlined, the end effect is generally a very wooden story.

Short stories usually do not have that many scenes, nor such complicated plots, that elaborate outlining is necessary. Certainly the writer must be exact about the background details of the story, especially science fictional elements when the story is set elsewhere from the here-and-now. And the protagonist's inner conflict must be nailed down firmly in the writer's mind before the first words are set on paper. But more often than not, a detailed outline of the plot stultifies the story. If you know your characters and their conflicts, you should let them write the story for you. Only if you find yourself drifting hopelessly at sea should you make a detailed outline for plotting purposes.

In writing stories of any length, the most important thing to keep in mind is *show, don't tell*. It is so important that I will say it again:

Show, don't tell.

This is especially true in the short story.

The moment you break the flow of the story's action to explain things to the reader, you run the risk of losing the reader. All of a sudden, instead of being in the story, living the role of the protagonist, the reader is listening to you lecturing. No matter how important the information you want to get across, readers are immediately reminded that they are *reading*, rather than living in the story. It is a risk that you should never run if you can avoid it. Never give the reader an opportunity to look up from the page.

If you find it necessary to explain the eighteen-century-long history of the Terran Confederation, find some way to have the characters do it for you. And not by having them discuss it! Putting dull lectures into dialogue form does not stop them from being dull lectures. If the story absolutely will not work without all that background history, you must *personify* the information in a character, and have that character's actions *show* the readers what you want them to learn.

In ninety-nine cases out of one hundred, all that background information can be chopped out of the story with no loss at all. The reader generally does not need or want long treatises of background information. The writer must know this information, because it will shape the actions of the story's characters. But in most cases, the story can get along perfectly well without the lecture, and the reader will be much happier without it.

If you are in doubt about this point, take a story you have written that has a large amount of background explanation in it, and remove the explanations. See for yourself if the story does not move more swiftly and keep your interest better. Of course, some of the characters' actions and motivations may be unexplained; but you should be able to find a way to explain them through action, rather than lecturing.

An important rule of thumb when it comes to imparting background information is never to allow the characters to tell each other anything that they already know. It is always tempting to explain things to the reader by using this technique, but it is always a mistake.

> "Why John," he said, "you remember how the expedition team got across Endless Swamp, don't you?"
>
> "Of course I do," John replied, chuckling softly. "They glued their snowshoes together to make a raft, and then . . ."

If you feel it absolutely necessary to get that particular point across to the reader, do it through action. Without even raising the question of the Endless Swamp Exploration Team, have John glance at a battered set of glued-together snowshoes hanging on the wall of his host's den. And even then, don't do it at all unless you are going to use those glued-together snowshoes later in the story. Like all background information, if it does not contribute to the story, throw it out.

Good writers are good plotters, although they seldom let a preconceived plot take such complete command of a story that it stiffens the characters and forces them into artificial situations. Mark Twain, one of the best writers America has produced, penned a marvelous essay about writing titled "Fenimore Cooper's Literary Offenses." It is funny, pointed, and contains more good advice about writing than any other sixteen pages in the English language.

Two important points that Twain raises about story construction are "that a tale shall accomplish something and arrive somewhere. [And] . . . that the episodes of a tale shall be necessary parts of the tale and shall help to develop it."

In other words, a story should have a beginning, a middle and an end. It is distressingly true that many, many slushpile stories lack such organization. They wander aimlessly, with no clear-cut purpose or conflict to give them shape and meaning. If you set your time bomb to go off at the end of the story and start it ticking on the first page, then almost inevitably the story will record your protagonist's attempts to prevent the explosion from destroying his life.

All the scenes and events in a short story must play a vital role. You do not have time or room to spend the first few pages describing the heroine's family background or the geological forces on the newly discovered planet Whatsit. Start the clock ticking! Delete every scene and every line of dialogue or description that does not contain a tick of the time bomb's clock in it! Be ruthless with your own prose. It is painful, well I know. But it is necessary.

Even in a novel, be wary of excursions from the main line that leads directly to that time bomb's explosion. Side trips are possible in a novel, perhaps even desirable, but they should be short and they should support the main plot line. More about that in chapter sixteen.

STORY MOVEMENT

As the plot develops, the story must *move*. That is, it must progress from the beginning, through the middle, to the end. In order for the story to move forward, the protagonist must learn things, grow and change. The reader must discover something new and, one hopes, something delightfully interesting or fiendishly frightening on every page.

Many new writers (and even some old hands, alas) confuse *motion* with *movement*. They whiz the protagonist out of his office, down a conveyer-belt slidewalk, into a jet helicopter, out to the spaceport, onto a shuttle rocket, and from there to the space station and finally to the antagonist's antigravity-driven starship—all in the name of movement. But if nothing is happening except a recitation of various modes of transportation, the story is not moving at all!

The characters can run breathlessly in circles page after page while the story stands still. The reader watches, bemused, as doors open and slam, engines roar, seatbelts get fastened—and nothing happens. If there is too much of this in a story, the reader will put it down and go off to the medicine chest for some Dramamine. Just as physical action is not necessarily conflict, physical motion is not necessarily movement.

A story moves forward when the protagonist (and consequently the reader) makes a new discovery. All the rest is busywork, no matter how much physical action or movement a writer includes in a story.

A good writer convinces the reader that the protagonist had a rich and busy life before the story began and will continue to do so after the last page of the story has been finished. In other words, the plot should be arranged so that the reader gets the feeling that this character is really alive; her life did not begin on page one and end on page last. She encompasses much more than merely the events of this one short story. Perhaps we shall meet her again, someday.

Of course, if the protagonist dies at the end of the story, the reader cannot expect to find him again. But there should be some character who *will* live on after the story's end, mourning for the protagonist. This provides a sense of continuity, which is a subtle but extremely powerful method for convincing the reader that the story is true.

A PLOT CHECKLIST

To recapitulate the points of this chapter:

1. Plant a time bomb on the first page — in the first paragraph, if possible.

2. Each story involves a race against time. That time bomb is set to explode at the climax of the story; its ticking should be heard on every page.

3. Every scene must further the plot. Especially in a short story, if a scene does not help move the story forward, take it out.

4. There should be surprises in the story every few pages. New complications and new problems should arise as the story progresses, moving the plot along on a chain of interlinked promises.

5. Show, don't tell!

6. The characters' actions should move the story from its be-

ginning to its end. Characters must be active, not passive. The protagonist must change.

7. The story ends when the time bomb goes off (or is prevented from going off). The ending must answer satisfactorily the major problems raised in the story's beginning.

8. Surprise endings are good only when the reader is truly surprised; even then they must be logically consistent with the rest of the story.

Chapter Thirteen

Plot in Science Fiction
The Shining Ones
A Complete Short Story

Johnny Donato lay flat on his belly in the scraggly grass and watched the strangers' ship carefully.

It was resting on the floor of the desert, shining and shimmering in the bright New Mexico sunlight. The ship was huge and round like a golden ball, like the sun itself. It touched the ground as lightly as a helium-filled balloon. In fact, Johnny wasn't sure that it really did touch the ground at all.

He squinted his eyes, but he still couldn't tell if the ship was really in contact with the sandy desert flatland. It cast no shadow, and it seemed to glow from some energies hidden inside itself. Again, it reminded Johnny of the sun.

But these people didn't come from anywhere near our sun, Johnny knew. *They come from a world of a different star.*

He pictured in his mind how small and dim the stars look at night. Then he glanced at the powerful glare of the sun. *How far away the stars must be!* And these strangers have traveled all that distance to come here. To Earth. To New Mexico. To this spot in the desert.

Johnny knew he should feel excited. Or maybe scared. But all he felt right now was curious. And hot. The sun was beating down on the rocky ledge where he lay watching, baking his bare arms and legs. He was used to the desert sun. It never bothered him.

But today something was burning inside Johnny. At first he thought it might be the sickness. Sometimes it made him feel hot and weak. But no, that wasn't it. He had the sickness, there was nothing anyone could do about that. But it didn't make him feel this way.

This thing inside him was something he had never felt before.

Maybe it was the same kind of thing that made his father yell in fury, ever since he had been laid off from his job. Anger was part of it, and maybe shame, too. But there was something else, something Johnny couldn't put a name to.

So he lay there flat on his belly, wondering about himself and the strange ship from the stars. He waited patiently, like his Apache friends would, while the sun climbed higher in the bright blue sky and the day grew hotter and hotter.

The ship had landed three days earlier. *Landed* was really the wrong word. It had touched down as gently as a cloud drifts against the tops of the mountains. Sergeant Warner had seen it. He just happened to be driving down the main highway in his State Police cruiser when the ship appeared. He nearly drove into the roadside culvert, staring at the ship instead of watching his driving.

Before the sun went down that day, hundreds of Army trucks and tanks had poured down the highway, swirling up clouds of dust that could be seen even from Johnny's house in Albuquerque, miles away. They surrounded the strange ship and let no one come near it.

Johnny could see them now, a ring of steel and guns. Soldiers paced slowly between the tanks, with automatic rifles slung over their shoulders. Pretending that he was an Apache warrior, Johnny thought about how foolish the Army was to make the young soldiers walk around in the heat instead of allowing them to sit in the shade. He knew that the soldiers were sweating and grumbling and cursing the heat. As if that would make it cooler. They even wore their steel helmets; a good way to fry their brains.

Each day since the ship had landed, exactly when the sun was highest in the sky, three strangers would step out of the ship. At least, that's what the people were saying back in town. The newspapers carried no word of the strangers, except front-page complaints that the Army wouldn't let news reporters or television camera crews anywhere near the starship.

The three strangers came out of their ship each day, for a few minutes. Johnny wanted to talk to them. Maybe—just maybe—they could cure his sickness. All the doctors he had ever seen just shook their heads and said that nothing could be done. Johnny would never live to be a full-grown man. But these strangers, if they really came from another world, a distant star, they might know how to cure a disease that no doctor on Earth could cure.

Johnny could feel his heart racing as he thought about it. He forced himself to stay calm. *Before you can get cured,* he told himself, *you've got to talk to the strangers. And before you can do that, you've got to sneak past all those soldiers.*

A smear of dust on the highway caught his eye. It was a State Police car, heading toward the Army camp. Sergeant Warner, most likely. Johnny figured that his mother had realized by now he had run away, and had called the police to find him. So he had another problem: avoid getting found by the police.

He turned back to look at the ship again. Suddenly his breath caught in his throat. The three strangers were standing in front of the ship. Without opening a hatch, without any motion at all. They were just there, as suddenly as the blink of an eye.

They were tall and slim and graceful, dressed in simple-looking coveralls that seemed to glow, just like their ship.

And they cast no shadows!

2

The strangers stood there for several minutes. A half-dozen people went out toward them, two in Army uniforms, the others in civilian clothes. After a few minutes the strangers disappeared. Just like that. Gone. The six men seemed just as stunned as Johnny felt. They milled around for a few moments, as if trying to figure out where the strangers had gone to. Then they slowly walked back toward the trucks and tanks and other soldiers.

Johnny pushed himself back down from the edge of the hill he was on. He sat up, safely out of view of the soldiers and police, and checked his supplies. A canteen full of water, a leather sack that held two quickly made sandwiches, and a couple of oranges. He felt inside the sack to see if there was anything else. Nothing except the wadded-up remains of the plastic wrap that had been around the other two sandwiches he had eaten earlier. The only other thing he had brought with him was a blanket to keep himself warm during the chill desert night.

There wasn't much shade, and the sun was getting really fierce. Johnny got to his feet and walked slowly to a clump of bushes that surrounded a stunted dead tree. He sat down and leaned his back against the shady side of the tree trunk.

For a moment he thought about his parents.

His mother was probably worried sick by now. Johnny often got up early and left the house before she was awake, but he always made sure to be back by lunchtime. His father would be angry. But he was always angry nowadays—most of the time it was about losing his job. But Johnny knew that what was really bugging his father was Johnny's own sickness.

Johnny remembered Dr. Pemberton's round red face, which was normally so cheerful. But Dr. Pemberton shook his head grimly when he told Johnny's father:

"It's foolish for you to spend what little money you have, John. Leukemia is incurable. You could send the boy to one of the research centers, and they'll try out some of the new treatments on him. But it won't help him. There is no cure."

Johnny hadn't been supposed to hear that. The door between the examination room where he was sitting and Dr. Pemberton's office had been open only a crack. It was enough for his keen ears, though.

Johnny's father sounded stunned. "But . . . he looks fine. And he says he feels okay."

"I know." Dr. Pemberton's voice sounded as heavy as his roundly overweight body. "The brutal truth, however, is that he has less than a year to live. The disease is very advanced. Luckily, for most of the time he'll feel fine. But towards the end . . ."

"These research centers," Johnny's father said, his voice starting to crack. "The scientists are always coming up with new vaccines . . ."

Johnny had never heard his father sound like that: like a little boy who had been caught stealing or something, and was begging for a chance to escape getting punished.

"You can send him to a research center," Dr. Pemberton said, slowly. "They'll use him to learn more about the disease. But there's no cure in sight, John. Not this year. Or next. And that's all the time he has."

And then Johnny heard something he had never heard before in his whole life: His father was crying.

They didn't tell him.

He rode back home with his father, and the next morning his mother looked as if she had been crying all night. But they never said a word to him about it. And he never told them that he knew.

Maybe it would have been different if he had a brother or sister to talk to. And he couldn't tell the kids at school, or his friends around the neighborhood. What do you say?

"Hey there, Nicko . . . I'm going to die around Christmas sometime."

No. Johnny kept silent, like the Apache he often dreamed he was. He played less and less with his friends, spent more and more of his time alone.

And then the ship came.

It had to *mean* something. A ship from another star doesn't just plop down practically in your back yard by accident.

Why did the strangers come to Earth?

No one knew. And Johnny didn't really care. All he wanted was a chance to talk to them, to get them to cure him. Maybe — who knew? — maybe they were here to find him and cure him!

He dozed off, sitting there against the tree. The heat was sizzling, there was no breeze at all, and nothing for Johnny to do until darkness. With his mind buzzing and jumbling a million thoughts together, his eyes drooped shut and he fell asleep.

"Johnny Donato!"

The voice was like a crack of thunder. Johnny snapped awake, so surprised that he didn't even think of being scared.

"Johnny Donato! This is Sergeant Warner. We know you're around here, so come out from wherever you're hiding."

Johnny flopped over on his stomach and peered around. He was pretty well hidden by the bushes that surrounded the tree. Looking carefully in all directions, he couldn't see Sergeant Warner or anyone else.

"Johnny Donato!" the voice repeated. "This is Sergeant Warner . . ."

Only now the voice seemed to be coming from farther away. Johnny realized that the State Police sergeant was speaking into an electric bullhorn.

Very slowly, Johnny crawled on his belly up to the top of the little hill. He made certain to stay low and keep in the scraggly grass.

Off to his right a few hundred yards was Sergeant Warner, slowly walking across the hot sandy ground. His hat was pushed back on his head, pools of sweat stained his shirt. He held the bullhorn up to his mouth, so that Johnny couldn't really see his face at all. The sergeant's mirror-shiny sunglasses hid the top half of his face.

Moving still farther away, the sergeant yelled into his bullhorn, "Now listen, Johnny. Your mother's scared half out of her mind. And your father doesn't even know you've run away — he's still downtown, hasn't come home yet. You come out now, you hear? It's hot out here, and I'm getting mighty unhappy about you."

Johnny almost laughed out loud. *What are you going to do, kill me?*

"Dammit, Johnny, I know you're around here! Now, do I have to call in other cars and the helicopter, just to find one stubborn boy?"

Helicopters! Johnny frowned. He had no doubts that he could hide from a dozen police cars and the men in them. But helicopters were something else.

He crawled back to the bushes and the dead tree and started scooping up loose sand with his bare hands. Pretty soon he was puffing and sweaty. But finally he had a shallow trench that was long enough to lie in.

He got into the trench and pulled his food pouch and canteen in with him. Then he spread the blanket over himself. By sitting up and leaning forward, he could reach a few small stones. He put them on the lower corners of the blanket to anchor them down. Then he lay down and pulled the blanket over him.

The blanket was brown and probably wouldn't be spotted from a helicopter. Lying there under it, staring at the fuzzy brightness two inches over his nose, Johnny told himself he was an Apache hiding out from the Army.

It was almost true.

It got very hot in Johnny's hideout. Time seemed to drag endlessly. The air became stifling; Johnny could hardly breathe. Once he thought he heard the drone of a helicopter, but it was far off in the distance. Maybe it was just his imagination.

He drifted off to sleep again.

Voices woke him up once more. More than one voice this time, and he didn't recognize who was talking. But they were very close by—they weren't using a bullhorn or calling out to him.

"Are you really sure he's out here?"

"Where else would a runaway kid go? His mother says he hasn't talked about anything but that weirdo ship for the past three days."

"Well, it's a big desert. We're never going to find him standing around here jabbering."

"I got an idea." The voices started to get fainter, as if the men were walking away.

"Yeah? What is it?"

Johnny stayed very still and strained his ears to hear them.

"Those Army guys got all sorts of fancy electronic stuff. Why don't we use them instead of walking around here frying our brains?"

"They had some of that stuff on the helicopter, didn't they?"

The voices were getting fainter and fainter.

"Yeah—but instead of trying to find a needle in a haystack, we ought to play it smart."

"What do you mean?"

Johnny wanted to sit up, to hear them better. But he didn't dare move.

"Why not set up the Army's fancy stuff and point it at the ship? That's where the kid wants to go. Instead of searching the whole damned desert for him . . ."

"I get it!" the other voice said. "Make the ship the bait in a mousetrap."

"Right. That's the way to get him."

They both laughed.

And Johnny, lying quite still in his hideaway, began to know how a starving mouse must feel.

3

After a long, hot, sweaty time Johnny couldn't hear any more voices or helicopter engines. And as he stared tiredly at the blanket over him, it seemed that the daylight was growing dimmer.

Must be close to sundown, he thought.

Despite his worked-up nerves, he fell asleep again. By the time he woke up, it was dark.

He sat up and let the blanket fall off to one side of his dugout shelter. Already it was getting cold.

But Johnny smiled.

If they're going to have all their sensors looking in toward the ship, he told himself, *that means nobody's out here. It ought to be easy to get into the Army camp and hide there. Maybe I can find someplace warm. And food!*

But another part of his mind asked, *And what then? How are you going to get from there to the ship and the strangers?*

"I'll cross that bridge when I come to it," Johnny whispered to himself.

Clutching the blanket around his shoulders for warmth in the chilly desert night wind, Johnny crept up to the top of the hill once more.

The Army tanks and trucks were still out there. A few tents had been set up, and there were lights strung out everywhere. It almost looked like a shopping center decorated for the Christmas season, there were so many lights and people milling around.

But the lights were glaring white, not the many colors of the holidays. And the people were soldiers. And the decorations were guns, cannon, radar antennas, lasers — all pointed inward at the strangers' ship.

The ship itself was what made everything look like Christmas, Johnny decided. It stood in the middle of everything, glowing and golden like a cheerful tree ornament.

Johnny stared at it for a long time. Then he found his gaze floating upward, to the stars. In the clear cold night of the desert, the stars gleamed and winked like thousands of jewels: red, blue, white. The hazy swarm of the Milky Way swung across the sky. Johnny knew there were billions of stars in the heavens, hundreds of billions, so many stars that they were uncountable.

"That ship came from one of them," he whispered to himself. "Which one?"

The wind moaned and sent a shiver of cold through him, despite his blanket.

Slowly, quietly, carefully, he got up and started walking down the hill toward the Army camp. He stayed in the shadows, away from the lights, and circled around the trucks and tanks. He was looking for an opening, a dark place where there was no one sitting around or standing guard, a place where he could slip in and maybe hide inside one of the trucks.

I wonder what the inside of a tank is like? he asked himself. Then he shook his head, as if to drive away such childish thoughts. He was an Apache warrior, he told himself, sneaking up on the Army camp.

He got close enough to hear soldiers talking and laughing among themselves. But still he stayed out in the darkness. He ignored the wind and cold, just pulled the blanket more tightly over his thin shoulders as he circled the camp. Off beyond the trucks, he could catch the warm yellow glow of the strangers' ship. It looked inviting and friendly.

And then there was an opening! A slice of shadow that cut between pools of light. Johnny froze in his tracks and examined the spot carefully, squatting down on his heels to make himself as small and undetectable as possible.

There were four tents set up in a row, with their backs facing Johnny. On one side of them was a group of parked trucks and jeeps. Metal poles with lights on them brightened that area. On the other side of the tents were some big trailer vans, with all sorts of antennas poking out of their roofs. That area was well lit too.

But the narrow lanes between the tents were dark with shadow. And Johnny could see no one around them. There were no lights showing from inside the tents, either.

Johnny hesitated only a moment or two. Then he quickly stepped up to the rear of one of the tents, poked his head around its corner and found no one in sight. So he ducked into the lane between the tents.

Flattening himself against the tent's vinyl wall, Johnny listened for sounds of danger. Nothing except the distant rush of the wind and the pounding of his own heart. It was dark where he was standing. The area seemed to be deserted.

He stayed there for what seemed like hours. His mind was saying that this was a safe place to hide. But his stomach was telling him that there might be some food inside the tents.

Yeah, and there might be some people inside there, too, Johnny thought.

His stomach won the argument. Johnny crept around toward the front of the tent. This area was still pretty well lit from the lamps over by the trucks and vans. Peeking around the tent's corner, Johnny could see plenty of soldiers sitting in front of the parking areas on the ground alongside their vehicles, eating food that steamed and somehow looked delicious, even from this distance. Johnny sniffed at the night air and thought he caught a trace of something filled with meat and bubbling juices.

Licking his lips, he slipped around the front of the tent and ducked inside.

It was dark, but enough light filtered through from the outside for Johnny to see that the tent was really a workroom of some sort. Two long tables ran the length of the tent. There were papers stacked at one end of one table, with a metal weight holding them in place. All sorts of instruments and gadgets were sitting on the tables: microscopes, cameras, something that looked sort of like a computer, other things that Johnny couldn't figure out at all.

None of it was food.

Frowning, Johnny went back to the tent's entrance. His stomach was growling now, complaining about being empty too long.

He pushed the tent flap back half an inch and peered outside. A group of men were walking in his direction. Four of them. One wore a soldier's uniform and had a big pistol strapped to his hip. The others wore ordinary clothes: slacks, windbreakers, jackets. One of them was smoking a pipe, or rather, he was waving it in his hand as he talked, swinging the pipe back and forth and pointing its stem at the glowing ship, then back at the other three men.

Johnny knew that if he stepped outside the tent now they would see him as clearly as anything.

Then he realized that the situation was even worse. They were heading straight for this tent!

4

There wasn't any time to be scared. Johnny let the tent flap drop back into place and dived under one of the tables. No place else to hide.

He crawled into the farthest corner of the tent, under the table, and huddled there with his knees pulled up tight against his nose and the blanket wrapped around him.

Sure enough, the voices marched straight up to the tent and the lights flicked on.

"You'd better get some sleep, Ed. No sense staying up all night again."

"Yeah, I will. Just want to go over the tapes from this afternoon one more time."

"Might as well go to sleep, for all the good *that's* going to do you."

"I know. Well . . . see you tomorrow."

"G'night."

From underneath the table, Johnny saw a pair of desert-booted feet walk into the tent. The man, whoever it was, wore striped slacks. He wasn't a soldier or a policeman, and that let Johnny breathe a little easier.

He won't notice me under here, Johnny thought. *I'll just wait until he leaves and . . .*

"You can come out of there now," the man's voice said.

Johnny froze. He didn't even breathe.

The man squatted down and grinned at Johnny. "Come on, kid. I'm not going to hurt you. I ran away from home a few times myself."

Feeling helpless, Johnny crawled out from under the table. He stood up slowly, feeling stiff and achy all of a sudden.

The man looked him over. "When's the last time you ate?"

"Around noontime."

Johnny watched the man's face. He had stopped grinning, and there were tight lines around his mouth and eyes that came from worry. Or maybe anger. He wasn't as big as Johnny's father, but he was solidly built. His hair was dark and long, almost down to his shoulders. His eyes were deep brown, almost black, and burning with some inner fire.

"You must be hungry."

Johnny nodded.

"If I go out to the cook van and get you some food, will you still be here when I come back?"

The thought of food reminded Johnny how hungry he really was. His stomach felt hollow.

"How do I know you won't bring back the State Troopers?" he asked.

The man shrugged. "How do I know you'll stay here and wait for me to come back?"

Johnny said nothing.

"Look kid," the man said, more gently, "I'm not going to hurt you. Sooner or later you're going to have to go home, but if you want to eat and maybe talk, then we can do that. I won't tell anybody you're here."

Johnny wanted to believe him. The man wasn't smiling; he seemed very serious about the whole thing.

"You've got to start trusting somebody, sooner or later," he said.

"Yeah . . ." Johnny's voice didn't sound very sure about it, even to himself.

"My name's Gene Beldone." He put his hand out.

Johnny reached for it. "I'm Johnny Donato," he said. Gene's grip was strong.

"Okay, Johnny." Gene smiled wide. "You wait here and I'll get you some food."

Gene came back in five minutes with an Army type of plastic tray heaped with hot, steaming food. And a mug of cold milk to wash it down. There were no chairs in the tent, but Gene pushed aside some of the instruments and helped Johnny to clamber up on the table.

For several minutes Johnny concentrated on eating. Gene went to the other table and fiddled around with what looked like a tape recorder.

"Did you really run away from home?" Johnny asked at last.

Gene looked up from his work. "Sure did. More than once. I know how it feels."

"Yeah."

"But . . ." Gene walked over to stand beside Johnny. "You know you'll have to go back home again, don't you?"

"I guess so."

"Your parents are probably worried. I thought I heard one of the State Troopers say that you were ill?"

Johnny nodded.

"Want to talk about it?"

Johnny turned his attention back to the tray of food. "No."

Gene gave a little one-shouldered shrug. "Okay. As long as you don't need any medicine right away, or anything like that."

Looking up again, Johnny asked, "Are you a scientist?"

"Sort of. I'm a linguist."

"Huh?"

"I study languages. The Army came and got me out of the university so I could help them understand the language the aliens speak."

"Aliens?"

"The men from the ship."

"Oh. Aliens—that's what you call them?"

"Right."

"Can you understand what they're saying?"

Gene grinned again, but this time it wasn't a happy expression. "Can't understand anything," he said.

"Nothing?" Johnny felt suddenly alarmed. "Why not?"

"Because the aliens haven't said anything to us."

"Huh?"

With a shake of his head, Gene said, "They just come out every day at high noon, stand there for a few minutes while we talk at them, and then pop back into their ship. I don't think they're listening to us at all. In fact, I don't think they're even looking at us. It's like they don't even know we're here!"

5

Gene let Johnny listen to the tapes of their attempts to talk to the aliens.

With the big padded stereo earphones clamped to his head, Johnny could hear the Army officers speaking, and another man that Gene said was a scientist from Washington. He could hear the wind, and a soft whistling sound, like the steady note of a telephone that's been left off the hook for too long. But no sounds at all from the aliens. No words of any kind, in any language.

Gene helped take the earphones off Johnny's head.

"They haven't said anything at all?"

"Nothing," Gene answered, clicking off the tape recorder. "The only sound to come from them is that sort of whistling thing—and that's coming from the ship. Some of the Army engineers think it's a power generator of some sort."

"Then we can't talk with them," Johnny suddenly felt very tired and defeated.

"We can talk *to* them," Gene said, "but I'm not even certain that they hear us. It's . . . it's pretty weird. They seem to look right through us — as if we're pictures hanging on a wall."

"Or rocks or grass or something."

"Right!" Gene looked impressed. "Like we're a part of the scenery, nothing special, nothing you'd want to talk to."

Something in Johnny was churning, trying to break loose. He felt tears forming in his eyes. "Then how can I tell them . . ."

"Tell them what?" Gene asked.

Johnny fought down his feelings. "Nothing," he said. "It's nothing."

Gene came over and put a hand on Johnny's shoulder. "So you're going to tough it out, huh?"

"What do you mean?"

Smiling, Gene answered, "Listen, kid. Nobody runs away from home and sneaks into an Army camp just for fun. At first I thought you were just curious about the aliens. But now . . . looks to me as if you've got something pretty big on your mind."

Johnny didn't reply, but — strangely — he felt safe with this man. He wasn't afraid of him anymore.

"So stay quiet," Gene went on. "It's *your* problem, whatever it is, and you've got a right to tell me to keep my nose out of it."

"You're going to tell the State Troopers I'm here?"

Instead of answering, Gene leaned against the table's edge and said, "Listen. When I was just about your age I ran away from home for the first time. That was in Cleveland. It was winter and there was a lot of snow. Damned cold, too. Now, you'd think that whatever made me leave home and freeze my backside in the snow for two days and nights — you'd think it was something pretty important, wouldn't you?"

"Wasn't it?"

Gene laughed out loud. "I don't know! I can't for the life of me remember what it was! It was awfully important to me then, of course. But now it's nothing, nowhere."

Johnny wanted to laugh with him, but he couldn't. "My problem's different."

"Yeah, I guess so," Gene said. But he was still smiling.

"I'm going to be dead before the year's over," Johnny said.

Gene's smile vanished. "What?"

Johnny told him the whole story. Gene asked several questions, looked doubtful for a while, but at last simply stood there looking very grave.

"That *is* tough," he said, at last.

"So I thought maybe the strangers—the aliens, that is—might do something, maybe cure it . . ." Johnny's voice trailed off.

"I see," Gene said. And there was real pain in his voice. "And we can't even get them to notice us, let alone talk with us."

"I guess it's hopeless then."

Gene suddenly straightened up. "No. Why should we give up? There must be something we can do!"

"Like what?" Johnny asked.

Gene rubbed a hand across his chin. It was dark with stubbly beard. "Well . . . maybe they do understand us and just don't care. Maybe they're just here sightseeing, or doing some scientific exploring. Maybe they think of us like we think of animals in a zoo, or cows in a field."

"But we're not animals!" Johnny said.

"Yeah? Imagine how we must seem to them." Gene began to pace down the length of the table. "They've traveled across lightyears—billions on billions of miles—to get here. Their ship, their brains, their minds must be thousands of years ahead of our own. We're probably no more interesting to them than apes in a zoo."

"Then why . . ."

"Wait a minute," Gene said. "Maybe they're not interested in us—but so far they've only seen adults, men, soldiers mostly. Suppose we show them a child, *you*, and make it clear to them that you're going to die."

"How are you going to get that across to them?"

"I don't know," Gene admitted. "Maybe they don't even understand what death is. Maybe they're so far ahead of us that they live for thousands of years—or they might even be immortal!"

Then he turned to look back at Johnny. "But I've had the feeling ever since the first time we tried to talk to them that they understand every word we say. They just don't *care*."

"And you think they'll care about me?"

"It's worth a try. Nothing else we've done has worked. Maybe this will."

6

Gene took Johnny to a tent that had cots and warm Army blankets.

"You get some sleep; you must be tired," he said. "I'll let the State Police know you're okay."

Johnny could feel himself falling asleep, even though he was only standing next to one of the cots.

"Do you want to talk to your parents? We can set up a radio-phone . . ."

"Later," Johnny said. "As long as they know I'm okay—I don't want to hassle with them until after we've talked to the aliens."

Gene nodded and left the tent. Johnny sat on the cot, kicked off his boots, and was asleep by the time he had stretched out and pulled the blanket up to his chin.

Gene brought him breakfast on a tray the next morning. But as soon as Johnny had finished eating and pulled his boots back on, Gene led him out to one of the big vans.

"General Hackett isn't too sure he likes our idea," Gene said as they walked up to the tan-colored van. It was like a civilian camper, only much bigger. Two soldiers stood guard by its main door, with rifles slung over their shoulders. It was already hot and bright on the desert, even though the sun had hardly climbed above the distant mountains.

The alien starship still hung in the middle of the camp circle, glowing warmly and barely touching the ground. For a wild instant, Johnny thought of it as a bright beach ball being balanced on a seal's nose.

Inside, the van's air conditioning was turned up so high that it made Johnny shiver.

But General Hackett was sweating. He sat squeezed behind a table, a heavy, fat-cheeked man with a black little cigar stuck in the corner of his mouth. It was not lit, but Johnny could smell its sour odor. Sitting around the little table in the van's main compartment were Sergeant Warner of the State Police, several civilians, and two other Army officers, both colonels.

There were two open chairs. Johnny and Gene slid into them.

"I don't like it," General Hackett said, shaking his head. "The whole world's going nuts over these weirdos, every blasted news-paper and TV man in the country's trying to break into this camp, and we've got to take a little kid out there to do our job for us? I don't like it."

Sergeant Warner looked as if he wanted to say something, but he satisfied himself with a stern glare in Johnny's direction.

Gene said, "We've got nothing to lose. All our efforts of the past three days have amounted to zero results. Maybe the sight of a youngster will stir them."

One of the civilians shook his head. A colonel banged his fist on the table and said, "By god, a couple rounds of artillery will stir them! Put a few shots close to 'em—make 'em know we mean business!"

"And run the risk of having them destroy everything in sight?" asked one of the civilians, his voice sharp as the whine of an angry hornet.

"This isn't some idiot movie," the colonel snapped.

"Precisely," said the civilian. "If we anger them, there's no telling how much damage they could do. Do you have any idea of how much energy they must be able to control in that ship?"

"One little ship? Three people?"

"That one little ship," the scientist answered, "has crossed distances billions of times greater than our biggest rockets. And there might be more than one ship, as well."

"NORAD hasn't picked up any other ships in orbit around Earth," the other colonel said.

"None of our radars have detected this ship," the scientist said, pointing in the general direction of the glowing starship. "The radars just don't get any signal from it at all!"

General Hackett took the cigar from his mouth. "All right, all right. There's no sense firing at them unless we get some clear indication that they're dangerous."

He turned to Gene. "You really think the kid will get them interested enough to talk to us?"

Gene shrugged. "It's worth a try."

"You don't think it will be dangerous?" the general asked. "Bringing him right up close to them like that?"

"If they want to be dangerous," Gene said, "I'll bet they can hurt anyone they want to, anywhere on Earth."

There was a long silence.

Finally General Hackett said, "Okay—let the kid talk to them."

Sergeant Warner insisted that Johnny's parents had to agree to the idea, and Johnny wound up spending most of the morning talking on the radio-phone in the sergeant's State Police cruiser. Gene talked to them too, and explained what they planned to do.

It took a long time to calm his parents down. His mother cried and said she was so worried. His father tried to sound angry about Johnny's running away. But he really sounded relieved that his son was all right. After hours of talking, they finally agreed to let Johnny face the aliens.

But when Johnny at last handed the phone back to Sergeant Warner, he felt lower than a scorpion.

"I really scared them," he told Gene as they walked back to the tents.

"Guess you did."

"But they wouldn't have let me go if I'd stayed home and asked them. They would've said no."

Gene shrugged.

Then Johnny noticed that his shadow had shrunk to practically nothing. He turned and squinted up at the sky. The sun was almost at zenith. It was almost high noon.

"Less than two minutes to noon," Gene said, looking at his wristwatch. "Let's get moving. I want to be out there where they can see you when they appear."

They turned and started walking out toward the aliens' ship. Past the trucks and jeeps and vans that were parked in neat rows. Past the tanks, huge and heavy, with the snouts of their long cannon pointed straight at the ship. Past the ranks of soldiers who were standing in neat files, guns cleaned and ready for action.

General Hackett and other people from the morning conference were sitting in an open-topped car. A corporal was at the wheel, staring straight at the ship.

Johnny and Gene walked out alone, past everyone and everything, out into the wide cleared space at the center of the camp.

With every step he took, Johnny felt more alone. It was as if he were an astronaut out on a spacewalk—floating away from his ship, out of contact, no way to get back. Even though it was hot, bright daylight, he could feel the stars looking down at him—one tiny, lonely, scared boy facing the unknown.

Gene grinned at him as they neared the ship. "I've done this four times now, and it gets spookier every time. My knees are shaking."

Johnny admitted, "Me too."

And then they were there! The three strangers, the aliens, standing about ten yards in front of Johnny and Gene.

It *was* spooky.

The aliens simply stood there, looking relaxed and pleasant. But they seemed to be looking right through Johnny and Gene. As if they weren't there at all.

Johnny studied the three of them very carefully. They looked completely human. Tall and handsome as movie stars, with broad shoulders and strong, square-jawed faces. The three of them looked enough alike to be brothers. They wore simple, silvery coveralls that shimmered in the sunlight.

They looked at each other as if they were going to speak. But they said nothing. The only sound Johnny could hear was that high-pitched kind of whistling noise that he had heard on tape the night before. Even the wind seemed to have died down, this close to the alien ship.

Johnny glanced up at Gene, and out of the corner of his eye, the three aliens seemed to shimmer and waver, as if he were seeing them through a wavy heat haze.

A chill raced along Johnny's spine.

When he looked straight at the aliens, they seemed real and solid, just like ordinary humans except for their glittery uniforms.

But when he turned his head and saw them only out of the corner of his eye, the aliens shimmered and sizzled. Suddenly Johnny remembered a day in school when they showed movies. His seat had been up close to the screen, and off to one side. He couldn't make out what the picture on the screen was, but he could watch the light shimmering and glittering on the screen.

They're not real!

Johnny suddenly understood that what they were all seeing was a picture, an image of some sort. Not real people at all.

And that, his mind was racing, *means that the aliens really don't look like us at all!*

7

"This is one of our children," Gene was saying to the aliens.

"He is not fully grown, as you can see. He has a disease that will . . ."

Johnny stopped listening to Gene. He stared at the aliens. They seemed so real when you looked straight at them. Turning his head toward Gene once more, he again saw that the aliens sparkled and shimmered. Like a movie picture.

Without thinking about it any further, Johnny suddenly sprang toward the aliens. Two running steps covered the distance, and he threw himself right off his feet at the three glittering strangers.

He sailed straight through them, and landed sprawled on his hands and knees on the other side of them.

"Johnny!"

Turning to sit on the dusty ground, Johnny saw that the aliens—or really, the images of them—were still standing there as if nothing had happened. Gene's face was shocked, mouth open, eyes wide.

Then the images of the aliens winked out. They just disappeared.

Johnny got to his feet.

"What did you do?" Gene asked, hurrying over to grab Johnny by the arm as he got to his feet.

"They're not real!" Johnny shouted with excitement. "They're just pictures . . . they don't really look like us. They're still inside the ship!"

"Wait, slow down," Gene said. "The aliens we've been seeing are images? Holograms, maybe. Yeah, that could explain . . ."

Looking past Gene's shoulder, Johnny could see a dozen soldiers hustling toward them. General Hackett was standing in his car and waving his arms madly.

Everything was happening so fast! But there was one thing that Johnny was sure of. The aliens—the *real* aliens, not the pretty pictures they were showing the Earthmen—the real aliens were still inside of their ship. They had never come out.

Then another thought struck Johnny. What if the ship itself was a picture, too? How could he *ever* talk to the star visitors, get them to listen to him, help him?

Johnny had to know. Once General Hackett's soldiers got to him, he would never get another chance to speak with the aliens.

With a grit of his teeth, Johnny pulled his arm away from

Gene, spun around, and raced toward the alien starship.

"Hey!" Gene yelled. "Johnny! No!"

The globe of the ship gleamed warmly in the sun. It almost seemed to pulsate, to throb like a living, beating heart. A heart made of gold, not flesh and muscle.

Johnny ran straight to the ship and, with his arms stretched out in front of him, he jumped at it. His eyes squeezed shut at the moment before he would hit the ship's shining hull.

Everything went black.

Johnny felt nothing. His feet left the ground, but there was no shock of hitting solid metal, no sense of jumping or falling or even floating. Nothing at all.

He tried to open his eyes, and found that he couldn't. He couldn't move his arms or legs. He couldn't even feel his heart beating.

I'm dead!

8

Slowly a golden light filtered into Johnny's awareness. It was like lying out in the desert sun with your eyes closed; the light glowed behind his closed eyelids.

He opened his eyes and found that he was indeed lying down, but not outdoors. Everything around him was golden and shining.

Johnny's head was spinning. He was inside the alien ship, he knew that. But it was unlike any spacecraft he had seen or heard of. He could see no walls, no equipment, no instruments; only a golden glow, like being inside a star—or maybe inside a cloud of shining gold.

Even the thing he was lying on, Johnny couldn't really make out what it was. It felt soft and warm to his touch, but it wasn't a bed or cot. He found that if he pressed his hands down hard enough, they would go into the golden glowing material a little way. Almost like pressing your fingers down into sand, except that this stuff was warm and soft.

He sat up. All that he could see was the misty glow, all around him.

"Hey, where are you?" Johnny called out. His voice sounded trembly, even though he was trying hard to stay calm. "I know you're in here someplace!"

Two shining spheres appeared before him. They were so bright that it hurt Johnny's eyes to look straight at them. They were like two tiny suns, about the size of basketballs, hovering in mid-air, shining brilliantly but giving off no heat at all.

"We are here."

It was a sound Johnny could hear. Somewhere in the back of his mind, despite his fears, he was a little disappointed. He had been half-expecting to "hear" a telepathic voice in his mind.

"Where are you?"

"You are looking at us." The voice was flat and unemotional. "We are the two shining globes that you see."

"You?" Johnny squinted at the shining ones. "You're the aliens?"

"This is our ship."

Johnny's heart started beating faster as he realized what was going on. He was inside the ship. And talking to the aliens!

"Why wouldn't you talk with the other men?" he asked.

"Why should we? We are not here to speak with them."

"What *are* you here for?"

The voice—Johnny couldn't tell which of the shining ones it came from—hesitated for only a moment. Then it answered, "Our purpose is something you could not understand. You are not mentally equipped to grasp such concepts."

A picture flashed into Johnny's mind of a chimpanzee trying to figure out how a computer works. *Did they plant that in my head?* he wondered.

After a moment, Johnny said, "I came here to ask for your help . . ."

"We are not here to help you," said the voice.

And a second voice added, "Indeed, it would be very dangerous for us to interfere with the environment of your world. Dangerous to you and your kind."

"But you don't understand! I don't want you to change anything, just—"

The shining one on the left seemed to bob up and down a little. "We do understand. We looked into your mind while you were unconscious. You want us to prolong your life span."

"Yes!"

The other one said, "We cannot interfere with the normal life processes of your world. That would change the entire course of your history."

"History?" Johnny felt puzzled. "What do you mean?"

The first sphere drifted a bit closer to Johnny, forcing him to shade his eyes with his hand. "You and your people have assumed that we are visitors from another star. In a sense, we are. But we are also travelers in time. We have come from millions of years in your future."

"Future?" Johnny felt weak. "Millions of years?"

"And apparently we have missed our target time by at least a hundred thousand of your years."

"Missed?" Johnny echoed.

"Yes," said the first shining one. "We stopped here—at this time and place—to get our bearings. We were about to leave when you threw yourself into the ship's defensive screen."

The second shining one added, "Your action was entirely foolish. The screen would have killed you instantly. We never expected any of you to attack us in such an irrational manner."

"I wasn't attacking you," Johnny said. "I just wanted to talk with you."

"So we learned, once we brought you into our ship and revived you. Still, it was a foolish thing to do."

"And now," the second shining sphere said, "your fellow men have begun to attack us. They assume that you have been killed, and they have fired their weapons at us."

"Oh no . . ."

"Have no fear, little one." The first sphere seemed almost amused. "Their primitive shells and rockets fall to the ground without exploding. We are completely safe."

"But they might try an atomic bomb," Johnny said.

"If they do, it will not explode. We are not here to hurt anyone, nor to allow anyone to hurt us."

A new thought struck Johnny. "You said your screen would have killed me. And then you said you brought me inside the ship and revived me. Was . . . was I dead?"

"Your heart had stopped beating," said the first alien. "We also found a few other flaws in your body chemistry, which we corrected. But we took no steps to prolong your life span. You will live some eighty to one hundred years, just as the history of your times has shown us."

Eighty to one hundred years! Johnny was thunderstruck. *The other flaws in body chemistry that they fixed—they cured the leukemia!*

Johnny was still staggered by the news, feeling as if he wanted to laugh and cry at the same time, when the first of the shining ones said:

"We must leave now, and hopefully find the proper time and place that we are seeking. We will place you safely among your friends."

"No! Wait! Take me with you! I want to go too!" Johnny surprised himself by shouting it, but he realized as he heard his own words that he really meant it. A trip through thousands of years of time, to who-knows-where!

"That is impossible, little one. Your time and place is here. Your own history shows that quite clearly."

"But you can't just leave me here, after you've shown me so much! How can I be satisfied with just one world and time when everything's open to you to travel to! I don't want to be stuck here-and-now. I want to be like you!"

"You will be, little one. You will be. Once we were like you. In time your race will evolve into our type of creature—able to roam through the universe of space and time, able to live directly from the energy of the stars."

"But that'll take millions of years."

"Yes. But your first steps into space have already begun. Before your life ends, you will have visited a few of the stars nearest to your own world. And, in the fullness of time, your race will evolve into ours."

"Maybe so," Johnny said, feeling downcast.

The shining one somehow seemed to smile. "No, little one. There is no element of chance. Remember, we come from your future. It has already happened."

Johnny blinked. "Already happened . . . you—you're really from Earth! Aren't you? You're from the Earth of a million years from now! Is that it?"

"Good-bye grandsire," said the shining ones together.

And Johnny found himself sitting on the desert floor in the hot afternoon sunlight, a few yards in front of General Hackett's command car.

"It's the kid! He's alive!"

Getting slowly to his feet as a hundred soldiers raced toward him, Johnny looked back toward the starship—the *time* ship.

It winked out. Disappeared. Without a sound or a stirring of the desert dust. One instant it was there, the next it was gone.

9

It was a week later that it really sank home in Johnny's mind.

It had been a wild week. Army officers quizzing him, medical doctors trying to find some trace of the disease, news reporters and TV interviewers asking him a million questions, his mother and father both crying that he was all right and safe and cured—a wild week.

Johnny's school friends hung around the house and watched from outside while the Army and news people swarmed in and out. He waved to them, and they waved back, smiling, friendly. They understood. The whole story was splashed all over the papers and TV, even the part about the leukemia. The kids understood why Johnny had been so much of a loner the past few months.

The President telephoned and invited Johnny and his parents to Washington. Dr. Gene Beldone went along too, in a private Air Force twin-engine jet.

As Johnny watched the New Mexico desert give way to the rugged peaks of the Rockies, something that the shining ones had said finally hit home to him:

You will live some eighty to one hundred years, just as the history of your times has shown us.

"How would they know about me from the history of these times?" Johnny whispered to himself as he stared out the thick window of the plane. "That must mean that my name will be famous enough to get into the history books, or tapes, or whatever they'll be using."

Thinking about that for a long time, as the plane crossed the Rockies and flew arrow-straight over the green farmlands of the Midwest, Johnny remembered the other thing that the shining ones had told him:

Before your life ends, you will have visited a few of the stars nearest to your own world.

"When they said you," Johnny whispered again, "I thought they meant us, the human race. But—maybe they really meant me! Me! I'm going to be an interstellar astronaut!"

For the first time, Johnny realized that the excitement in his life hadn't ended. It was just beginning.

Chapter Fourteen

Plot in Science Fiction
Plot: Practice

Character gives us qualities, but it is in actions—what we do—that we are happy or the reverse. . . . All human happiness and misery take the form of action.
—*Aristotle*

A s noted in chapter twelve, the time bomb in "Fifteen Miles" is a countdown that will end with the success or failure of Kinsman's efforts to save the priest, plus the success or failure of his efforts to keep his secret to himself. In "Sepulcher," there are actually three time bombs: Elverda's confrontation with the alien artwork (and her own approaching death), her realization that the corporate wars must be stopped, and her understanding of what the alien artwork truly is. "Crisis of the Month" was much simpler. The time bomb was the need to find a crisis, a need complicated by the protagonist's temptations.

Each of these plots took a different form. In "Fifteen Miles," where the lunar environment served as the antagonist, the plot followed Kinsman's physical struggle to bring the injured priest back to safety. It was a physical struggle that mirrored his inner emotional turmoil.

The plot of "Sepulcher" can be thought of as an inside-out version of the plot for "Fifteen Miles." Instead of a physical journey across harshly hostile terrain, the characters in "Sepulcher" are moving deeper and deeper inward—both physically, into the heart of the asteroid, and emotionally, into their innermost cores.

"Crisis of the Month" has the simplest plot. The time bomb starts ticking on the first page. The CCC must find a crisis to feed to the news media. Two complications arise, both involving the protagonist, Tom James: He is being tempted by Mary Richards and he wants to advance his career. The plot is a simple straight line. When Tom resolves one of his problems, he resolves all of them.

The plot of "The Shining Ones" is also very simple, although the story is much longer than the others. It consists of a series of barriers that Johnny Donato must get through, each barrier being more difficult to penetrate than the one that preceded it.

I started, as with so many stories, with a protagonist, in this case, a twelve-year-old boy. What was his problem, the conflict that would drive him, the time bomb that would tick until the story's climax?

It is unusual and unrealistic for a boy so young to have an implacable enemy who threatens his life. And make no mistake about it, stories in which the protagonist's life is threatened are the strongest stories. So Johnny had to be threatened by an illness that would be fatal. Leukemia fit the requirement; it attacks young people, predominantly, and although it is almost always fatal, it does not incapacitate the victim until very near the end of its course. Therefore, Johnny could have the fatal disease but still get around and do the things he needed to do.

Once the time bomb has started ticking, it is necessary to show the reader some hope of reaching it in time to prevent the explosion. That hope became the alien ship, and Johnny's stubborn belief that the aliens could—and would—cure him.

Now the writing task came to be setting up the barriers between Johnny and his one chance of being cured. As the story was being written, I was somewhat surprised to see the barriers rising like concentric ringwalls, each of them centered on the golden glowing ship and the aliens within it.

The first barrier had already been hurdled by Johnny before page one of the story. That was his parents. Johnny had already run away from home when the story opens. It was not necessary to show that, mainly because it would add nothing to the story's progress. Besides, it gives the reader the feeling that Johnny's life began before the story started; this helps to convince the reader that Johnny is really alive.

The desert itself is something of a barrier, but one that Johnny crosses rather easily. Then comes the State Police, first in the person of Sergeant Warner, then in a helicopter, and finally as a couple of searching officers. Johnny eludes them all. Next is the Army camp, drawn up in a circle around the aliens' glowing ship. Johnny slips past the guards and gets inside the camp.

To allow Johnny to succeed even further by himself, without help, would have been stretching the reader's credulity too far, I thought. Besides, there comes a point in a story where you need a second character to give depth and variety; you can't have the protagonist talking to himself all the time, especially in a story that is going to be more than a few thousand words long.

So Gene Beldone enters the scene. He comes in first as another test for Johnny, another barrier, perhaps. But he quickly turns into a friend and ally. The next barrier is the general, and Gene helps Johnny to get past him.

Notice that by the time we meet the ultimate barrier, the aliens themselves, we have already planted the fact that they are uncommunicative. The aliens are here for their own purposes, not to help a sick human youngster. That should make the reader feel that perhaps Johnny's labors so far have been all in vain. Neither the reader nor the protagonist should ever get the feeling everything will turn out all right. If the protagonist has to sweat out the solution to the story's basic problem, the reader will sweat too. And not be bored.

PLANTING TECHNIQUES

This business of *planting* is an important part of good plotting. You cannot have important twists in a story suddenly pop up out of nowhere, with no preparation for them beforehand. The reader has got to be surprised, but not startled or puzzled by totally unexpected twists of events.

If the protagonist is being held at gunpoint by the antagonist and distracts his attention by knocking over a milk bottle, the writer should have planted that milk bottle in that place during an earlier scene, or at least earlier in the same scene. You cannot have the milk bottle suddenly appear just for the convenience of the hero. The reader will immediately conclude that the author is making life too easy for the protagonist.

There is another side to the technique of planting. If you have an ornate dueling pistol sitting on a character's desk in an early scene of your story, it had better be fired sometime later. Otherwise, there is no purpose to it, but the reader will constantly be wondering what it was doing there and when it will appear again. Such a prop takes on the significance of another ticking time bomb, as far as the reader is concerned, and you dare not disappoint your reader. If the gun plays no part in the story, then get rid of it and don't mention it. Do not clutter up a story — especially a short story — with unneeded props and plants. You may think you are fascinating the readers with rich detail, but all you are doing is teasing them with promises that you have no intention of keeping.

In "The Shining Ones," the aliens' lack of communication with the humans was the ultimate barrier. Johnny gets past that by giving everything he has, including his very life, to break through to the aliens. He succeeds in doing so, only to be told that they will not help him.

But, like the prophecies of the three witches in *Macbeth*, the words that the aliens speak actually mean something very different from the meaning that Johnny at first attaches to them. In essence, this play on words becomes something of a barrier, too, and hides the fact of Johnny's success until the dramatically opportune moment.

If the story had ended at this point, it would have seemed rather anticlimactic and dull: Boy has problem, boy works on problem, boy solves problem. Ho-hum. The reader expects something more, something to lift the tale out of the ordinary, something surprising or even exalting, over and beyond the bare solution to the original problem.

It was tempting to try to show much more about the aliens. But that was a dangerous step. For one thing, this is Johnny's story, not theirs. For another, they are much more interesting if they're kept somewhat mysterious. And, frankly, the third factor was that Johnny and the aliens worked out this problem pretty much for themselves. I found myself reading the manuscript as it came out of the typewriter, about as surprised as any reader can be.

We learn a little bit about the aliens, enough to startle us and make us eager for more. They are not really aliens, after all; they are our own descendants, from millions of years in the future, evolved as far beyond our present human form as we have evolved beyond the tree shrews who were our ancestors.

And it turns out that Johnny has not only been cured of his leukemia, but he has deduced that he will become an astronaut and undertake missions to other stars. His life will go on; he will become a famous historical figure. This is the ultimate reward for his courage and determination: not merely survival, but glory.

It may be that all these techniques and surprises were obvious to you as you read the story. If so, then the framework of the plot was not covered well enough by the action, characterizations and background. If the reader can see the machinery working behind each page, then the story can hardly be holding her interest. But if the reader turns over the final page, looks up and blinks with surprise that she is not still in the story, and returns to the real world with something of a jolt—then the writer has done a very good job, indeed.

REVIEW OF THE PLOT CHECKLIST

1. **Plant a time bomb on the first page—in the first paragraph, if possible.** In the first paragraph of "The Shining Ones" we see that a strange ship has landed in the desert. By the middle of the first page we know that Johnny is the protagonist of this story and that the ship may have come from the stars. By the end of the page we learn that Johnny has a serious illness, although it is not named as leukemia until later. The time bomb is ticking loudly and clearly from page 1 onward.

2. **Each story involves a race against time.** That time bomb is set to explode at the climax of the story; its ticking should be heard on every page. As Johnny struggles to get through the barriers between himself and the alien visitors, we learn that the aliens are uncommunicative, Johnny's illness will be fatal, he has run away from home, and the State Police are searching for him. Each page adds a new level of difficulty for our struggling protagonist.

3. **Every scene must further the plot.** Especially in a short story, if a scene does not help move the story forward, take it out. Go through the story, scene by scene. Jot down the key piece of information that each scene gives you. Try to find a scene that does not further the plot.

4. **There should be surprises in the story every few pages.** New complications and new problems should arise as the story

progresses, moving the plot along on a chain of interlinked promises. The interlinked promises (or problems) are obviously the barriers that lie between Johnny and his goal of being cured by the aliens. As the story progresses, those problems lead to surprises: Johnny evades detection by the police helicopter; Gene Beldone turns into an ally; Johnny discovers that the aliens are merely holographic images. Look for the other surprises in the story and try to remember how you felt when you first came across them.

5. **Show, don't tell!** It is virtually impossible to write a story without giving the reader any background information at all. But pay particular attention to the flashback scene in the doctor's office. I could have simply told the reader that Johnny has an incurable case of leukemia. Instead I inserted a scene that shows how Johnny — and his father — felt when they first heard the diagnosis. That is the difference between showing and telling. If a piece of information is important enough to be included in the story, it is probably important enough to warrant at least a brief scene to show it.

6. **The characters' actions should move the story from its beginning to its end. Characters must be active, not passive. The protagonist must change.** Johnny is certainly active! He works hard, struggles to succeed, makes discoveries about the aliens and about himself. In the course of his story he changes from a frightened runaway facing death by leukemia to a lad on his way to the White House — and the stars.

7. **The story ends when the time bomb goes off (or is prevented from going off). The ending must answer satisfactorily the major problems raised in the story's beginning.** In "The Shining Ones" the protagonist is struggling to save his life. The time bomb is that deadly case of leukemia that threatens Johnny. He succeeds in preventing that time bomb from destroying him. And in doing so, he achieves much more than he — or the reader — dared hope for.

8. **Surprise endings are good only when the reader is truly surprised; even then they must be logically consistent with the rest of the story.** There is a surprise at the end of the story. Johnny is not merely cured, he will become an interstellar astronaut. The surprise is entirely consistent with the rest of the story,

however, and therefore should be satisfying to the reader. Were you surprised? Were you satisfied?

While this chapter and chapter twelve have concentrated on plotting short fiction, in chapter sixteen some further aspects of plotting the novel are discussed.

Chapter Fifteen

Think Before You Write: Preparing for the Novel

The only reason for the existence of a novel is that it does attempt to represent life. . . . The only obligation to which we in advance may hold a novel . . . is that it be interesting.

—Henry James

At first glance, you might think that writing a novel is pretty much like writing a short story, only longer.

Well, yes. And no.

Everything we have discussed so far in this book—character, background, conflict and plot—applies to the writing of novels as much as to shorter fiction. (There are several classes of short fiction, loosely based on word length: the short-short story [no more than 2,000 words], the short story [generally up to 7,500 words], the novelette [20,000-25,000 words], and the novella, which in form is often a short novel.) Yet the novel is truly a different entity. It is not merely the novel's greater length that makes it so different from shorter fiction. The novel is (or should be) deeper and more complex than the typical short story. This combination of greater length, psychological depth, and complexity of plot means that the writer must spend much more time on a novel than on a short story. The novel is fundamentally different not merely in length, but it is different in almost every aspect.

Writing a novel is a long siege, and if you are not prepared to spend weeks, months, even years on the same work, you are not ready to write a novel.

In fact, most writers find fairly early in their careers that they are either novelists or short-story writers. It is not that the novelist can write only novels and finds it impossible to do anything shorter, or that the short-story writer never even attempts a novel. But the professional writers that I know find themselves much more comfortable on one side of that line than the other.

I myself am a novelist. I feel quite at home writing stories that take up five hundred manuscript pages or more. I write short fiction, too, occasionally; four of my shorter works are reprinted in this book. But for me, a short story is something I write rarely. I have no idea why. I began as a teenager by writing short stories, but by the time I was eighteen I was already working on my first novel, and I have spent most of my career writing novels ever since.

FINANCIAL REWARDS

When it comes to money, novels usually are a better investment of the writer's time and effort.

A short story may sell for anything from a few dollars to a few thousand, depending on which magazine or anthology buys it. A novel will usually earn its author an advance from the publisher of at least several thousand dollars. (An advance is money paid by the publisher to the writer before the book is published. The writer usually receives part of the advance upon signing the contract with the publisher and the remainder when the manuscript is accepted by the editor. Recently, publishers have been breaking the advance into three or more parts, with the final payment coming when the book is actually published. Technically, advances are against royalties; the advanced money is subtracted from the book's royalty income until the advance is cleared.)

Five-figure advances are commonplace. Well-established authors garner advances of hundreds of thousands, even millions!

Those very large advances are as rare as total eclipses of the sun, true enough. But even the more modest advances are usually far more than the best short-story sale will earn. Of course, it takes much longer to write a novel than a short story. But if the novel continues to sell it can earn royalties for years, while generally a short story can be sold only once. Even if a story is reprinted for an anthology, it earns only a fraction of what a novel would.

Based on a wage of dollars earned per hours spent writing, novels are probably much better earners than short stories. Remember that time is the only natural resource a writer possesses.

It is important to make the best use of your time.

Having said all that, I must add that writers do not live on money alone. If you are more comfortable and more productive writing short stories, do not force yourself to try a novel merely because you think it will earn more for you. Be happy in your work! If you are a natural short-story writer, stay with it. Better to write good short stories than a bad novel, especially if your novel never gets published, and the time you put into it is lost.

THE LONG ROAD TO THE NOVEL

When someone asks me, "How long did it take you to write your latest book?" I am always at a loss for an answer.

What the questioner means, I am certain, is, How long did it take to put down all the words that comprise the novel? But the physical act of writing is not the whole job of creating a novel — or a shorter work of fiction, either, for that matter. In most cases, the time spent actually putting the words on paper is the *least* amount of time spent on the project.

It may take months or years to type out the words of a full-length novel. Almost invariably, it takes the author much longer to arrive at the point where he can sit down and begin writing. Actually, the proper answer to "How long did it take you to write your book?" is this: "All my life."

During World War II it took more than two years for the Allies to plan the D-Day invasion of Normandy. More than two years of planning, building up supplies, training men, preparing the detailed tactics — all for one single day's battle.

Similarly, it takes months or years of thinking, planning, organizing, plotting, developing characters, researching the background, and bringing into focus all the other details of a novel before you are ready to begin writing. Even so, the first draft of a novel can be agonizing.

For me, that first draft is rather like meeting a group of strangers on a bare stage in an empty theater. I have a rough idea of what I want them to say and do, but as yet we have no script, no props, no sets. At some point, though, I begin to get familiar and comfortable with my characters, and they begin to move and act on their own. Then it is as if I am not actually writing the novel, the characters are writing it for me. My fingers move across the keyboard, and I read the story as it appears, just as surprised as any other reader would be.

But before I (or any writer) can get to that point, there is an enormous amount of thinking and planning to do.

The most obvious difference between a novel and shorter fiction is that the novel's greater length allows—indeed, demands—greater depth and complexity. Where a short story generally illuminates a single incident, the novel can tell the tale of a whole lifetime, even several generations of lifetimes. The novelist can deal with a larger cast of characters and more intricate interactions among those characters. Because of this greater complexity, and because it usually takes months, if not years, to complete a novel, it is virtually impossible to carry the entire story in your head. You need notes, outlines, sketches and other aids. Like a good general preparing for a crucial battle, you must build up your logistical supplies, train your troops, scout the terrain, and plan your tactics with great care.

THE DESK BOOK

All the material that goes into your novel can be organized into a desk book. In years gone by I used a three-ring loose-leaf binder; now my desk book is a set of files in my computer. (Always back up every computer file. Protect yourself against losing your irreplaceable notes and drafts by backing up everything. As a grizzled newspaper veteran told me once, back in the days when we used typewriters, "Only an idiot doesn't make carbon copies of his work.")

The reason for the loose-leaf book was flexibility. I could insert new pages and shuffle pages around to suit whatever organization I wanted. The computer allows me to do this even more easily. But I still carry a pocket-sized notebook with me wherever I go, just in case an idea strikes me while I'm away from my computer. When I am going to be away from home for several days, often I bring a notebook computer with me, with the novel and all my notes in it.

While writers have individual ideas about what should go into the desk book, at a minimum your book should contain sections on characters, names, background information, lines and phrases, and a chart of character appearances.

Characters. This is where you put your character sketches, which can range from a simple *emotion* vs. *emotion* equation as we discussed in chapter two, to a full-blown biography that reaches back to grandparents or even beyond.

Physical descriptions are important. Everything from the color of the protagonist's hair to her shoe size should be included here. What does your protagonist like for breakfast? What is her mother's maiden name? Psychological understanding is even more important. Here in the character sketches you must describe the emotional conflicts that drive your major characters; you must write down each character's strengths and weaknesses. Especially for the major characters of the novel, you should know everything there is to know, and you should write it all down in as much detail as possible.

Keep adding to the sketches as new ideas and fresh information come to mind. Even while you are writing the novel, add every new detail to the character sketches. Later in the novel you may need to know what Mary's mother died of. It will be much easier to check your desk book notes than to go paging through the novel itself until you locate the scene where you mentioned the old lady's demise.

Not all the information that you put into the sketches will get into the pages of your novel. Most of the details in the character sketches are important for you, the author, to know, but probably irrelevant or even boring to the reader. It is just as important to know what to leave out of a story as what to put in. But while you are in the early stages of collecting your thoughts and your notes, put down everything that occurs to you. Every blessed thing. You never know which trivial point will become crucially important to you six months downstream. And then keep on jotting down new information. Today's note may be the backbone for chapter nineteen. Or just the right touch needed for the last page of the novel, for that matter.

Names. Not just the names of your major characters, not merely the names of all the characters in your plot outline. Write down every name you run across that sounds interesting to you. Some names will evoke a character in your mind. What does "Mitch Westover" suggest to you? Or "Bunny Wunderly"? Even if you do not use those characters in this novel, they may become valuable on a later project.

Especially if your novel is going to include foreigners or people of various nationalities, keep your eyes peeled for exotic names. The daily newspaper is a good source. Each news story from overseas has a treasure trove of foreign names in it. Write them all down in your desk book.

Include more than character names in the desk book. Family names are important. So are names of cities, rivers, mountains, hotels, songs, museums—everything that goes into your novel will have a name. And since you do not know which will go into the story and which will be left out, err on the side of generosity. Be sensitive to names and put them down where you can find them when you need them.

Lines and Phrases. In this section of the desk book jot down quotations you may want to use, lines of dialogue that pop into your head, ideas for scenes, bits of description, etc.

When I first heard Rimsky-Korsakov's symphonic suite *Scheherazade*, as a teenager, its second movement painted a vivid scene in my mind. Thirty-some years later I began work on a novel called *Colony*. I simply jotted down the word *Scheherazade* in my desk book. Not only did that music-inspired scene make up chapter two in its entirety, the scene gave me the backbone for the novel and for one of its three major characters, the daughter of a rich and powerful sheik who is secretly "Scheherazade," the leader of a worldwide revolutionary movement.

Chart of Character Appearances. It takes a long time to write a novel. I know that some have been dashed off in a weekend, but we are talking now about *your* novel, a task that you are serious about, not a weekend's piece of hack work.

Once you begin to write the novel, its very length and complexity may cause trouble for you. Over the weeks and months that you work at it, you may become lost in the twists of the plot or simply forget vital details. This can bog down your writing effort, or discourage you so badly you stop writing altogether.

One simple way to prevent this from happening is to draw up a chart of character appearances. The chart is simplicity itself: Just write the chapter numbers across the top of the page and jot down the names of the characters down the left margin. As you work, add more chapters and more character names.

Now run vertical lines between the chapter numbers and horizontal lines between the character names. You have created a chart.

When a character appears in a chapter, put a star along that character's line in the box beneath the number of the chapter. If the character is only mentioned in the chapter, use a dot or a check mark. If the character does not appear and is not mentioned, leave the box blank. If the character dies, put an X in the appropriate box.

This chart does several things for you. At a glance you can tell which of your characters are appearing the most; perhaps one you thought would be a minor character is popping up in almost every chapter. Time to start thinking about why that character seems to be taking on a larger role than you had first assigned. Perhaps several chapters go by without your protagonist making an appearance; time to think about just whose story you are telling.

The chart also tells you which characters are interacting with one another by appearing in the same chapters. Conversely, it shows which characters are not interacting with one another, thereby suggesting ways to bring new interactions, new relationships, new conflicts into the novel.

The Plot Outline

Beginning writers are almost invariably told to outline their novels before they start trying to write them. I am not certain that this is always good advice, although outlining the novel will undoubtedly help to organize your thoughts and ideas. The problem is that sometimes the writer relies too much on the outline and is afraid to deviate from it, even when the characters are telling the writer that they want to break free of its strictures.

No two writers outline in the same manner, and even an individual may change the way he outlines the plot of a novel. In my own case, I began with very tight outlines that covered every chapter and every scene from beginning to end of the novel. I quickly learned that this was too confining; it left no room for my characters to grow and change and take over the story for themselves. So, today, my outlines are minimal, bare bones, just enough to suggest where the story begins and in what direction it is heading. Once I begin writing the novel, I seldom consult the outline. For me, it is much more important to know the protagonist, the antagonist and their fundamental conflict than to have a plan of each chapter and scene in hand. If the characters are interesting and their conflict vital, they write the novel for me, and I do not need an outline at all.

I have been at this business for more than forty years, however. If you are starting your first novel, you might feel uneasy without an outline to refer to.

How detailed should your outline be? As detailed as you need it to be. If you feel comfortable just jotting down a few lines, then hitting the keyboard, fine. But chances are that you will either run out of steam within a few days or weeks, or your novel will start to wander away from the direction you first set for it. An outline would have helped in either case.

When you begin a plot outline, there are five key points you must address:

1. Who are the novel's protagonist and antagonist?
2. Where does the novel begin?
3. Complications.
4. Climax.
5. Resolution.

1. Who is the protagonist? Who is the antagonist? What is their conflict? The conflict between these two characters will define your story; it is the central issue of the plot.

The antagonist may be nature or society, but even then it is best to represent these nonhuman forces by human characters. In my novel *The Winds of Altair*, a team of pioneers is sent to a newly discovered planet to prepare it for colonization from Earth. The planet is wildly inhospitable for human habitation; the pioneers' mission is to make it Earthlike. But to do so, they must wipe out the native life forms. The protagonist is a young man, barely out of his teens. The antagonist is the savage natural environment of the planet—and the society back on Earth that demands the destruction of this new world's native ecology. I personified the planet's ecology by turning one of its brute animals into a major character. And the demanding society of Earth was personified by the commander of the pioneers, an inflexible, petty tyrant.

2. Where does the story begin? Usually it is best to begin in the middle of the action, to get the story off to an irresistible start. Like soldiers jumping into their drop zone from a hovering helicopter, you want to hit the ground running. The background and biographical details can be filled in later.

An excellent example of how this is done is Mario Puzo's *The Godfather*. He starts with Don Corleone at the peak of his power; only after you are so engrossed in the novel that you cannot put it down does Puzo show you the Godfather's earlier years.

3. What complications develop? These complications, new problems that arise as the story unfolds, will undoubtedly involve other characters. In Dashiell Hammett's classic *The Maltese Falcon*, detective Sam Spade meets an exotic assortment of characters, from the beautiful Brigid O'Shaughnessy to the mysterious Joel Cairo to the aptly named fat man, Gutman. Each character brings new conflicts and new problems into the novel.

4. What is the climax of the novel? When is the time bomb set to explode and what happens when the clock ticks down to that point? My own novel *Millennium* (now part of *The Kinsman Saga*) was set in the month of December 1999. Global nuclear war is imminent. The climax comes on the last day of the year, New Year's Eve, when a mob attacks and burns the United Nations building in New York City while the protagonist, Chet Kinsman, struggles to keep the world from incinerating itself.

5. What is the resolution of the story? Who wins, who loses? Just as in a short story, the resolution must satisfy the reader with its logic and its justice to the protagonist. Yet it should surprise the reader, too, with a conclusion that the reader did not foresee. In *Millennium* the world changes. Kinsman gives his life not merely to avert nuclear war, but to create the beginnings of a new world order in which war will become impossible.

The value of an outline is to organize your thoughts well enough so that you feel confident you can write the novel. If you can put those five points on paper, you should have enough knowledge about your characters and their story to begin the long process of writing.

Perhaps you feel you need more. All right, you can make a detailed outline, chapter by chapter, in which you write down the characters that appear in each scene, the location of each scene, and what each scene is supposed to accomplish in the way of moving the plot along. If that sounds like a daunting task, you can learn how easy (and interesting) it is by taking someone else's published novel and writing an outline for it — chapter by chapter, scene by scene. That will teach you how to organize your own outline; it may even help you learn how to write your novel.

Once you begin writing, though, let the characters take over and forget about the outline. Keep it close at hand in case you get stuck; it may help to refer back to your original conception if you have lost your way. But if all is going well and the characters are surprising you at every turn, enjoy the sensation and keep the outline out of sight. But within reach.

PLOT STRUCTURE

Every story's plot has a structure. Consider *Cinderella*, for example, the ultimate success story: Poor, maltreated girl goes to royal ball (with some magical help), has the prince fall in love with her, and, after a few complications, weds the prince and lives happily ever after.

If you drew a graph to illustrate the plot structure of *Cinderella*, it could be represented by a line that starts out flat and then swings upward. The point at which the upward curve begins is the point in the story where the reader begins to feel that everything will turn out well for Cindy, most likely when the Fairy Godmother first appears.

Now consider *Hamlet*. A graph of this play's plot would be a downward curve, with a short flat section at the beginning, and the descending arc starting when the ghost of Hamlet's father tells Hamlet that he was murdered by his brother, Claudius, who has now married his widow, Hamlet's mother. The rest of the play leads inevitably to the final tragic climax and conclusion.

Thinking about that downer curve, imagine now rewriting Shakespeare's play so that Claudius gives his throne to Hamlet and voluntarily exiles himself to a monastery where he will spend the rest of his days doing penance for his sins. A happy ending! The downward curve suddenly reverses course and swings upward again. It looks fishy, artificial. And it is. Pinning such a falsely happy ending onto the tragedy of *Hamlet* is like having Cinderella commit suicide just as the prince is taking her home to his castle.

When I was editing magazines, I often received manuscripts in which the writer set up an interesting plot but then did not know how to resolve it, except to kill off the protagonist. Suicide is sometimes called the coward's way out of life's problems; killing the protagonist because you don't know how else to end the story is the cowardly writer's way out.

Novels have much more plot structure than short fiction, and it is very helpful to sit down and draw a graph of the plot you are developing for your novel.

As we have already seen, the plot of a novel might be the simple upward curve of a story with a happy ending or the inescapable downward curve of a tragedy. An hourglass figure is also possible when you start with two very different characters and, through their interaction, they change their lives dramatically. One may go from being evil to being good, while the other sinks from goodness to evil. Or a poor man might find wealth and happiness while his rich counterpart becomes destitute and miserable.

Mark Twain's *The Prince and the Pauper* deals with two boys who look alike switching their roles in medieval England. In my novel *The Dueling Machine*, I developed a variation of the hourglass plot. My protagonist was a good-natured, bumbling oaf; the antagonist a nearly perfect warrior. At the story's climax the two men merge their personalities: Each gains such a profound insight into the other that they come out of the story closer than brothers. The hourglass, in this case, was altered into something more like an upside-down wine glass, with the two curves merging to form a united single line.

A circular plot line is one where the story ends up where it began. In L. Frank Baum's *The Wizard of Oz*, Dorothy goes through marvelous adventures but ends up exactly where she began, in her home in Kansas—albeit with a new appreciation of how dear her home and family are to her. You can generate a variation of the circular plot by using two separate characters, or two separate themes, and having them meet and separate and meet again. The resulting plot line can look like a figure eight or like a double spiral, if you have the two lines meeting and separating many times.

Then there is the episodic novel, such as *Don Quixote* or Dickens's *The Pickwick Papers*. At first glance such novels may look like nothing more than a series of short adventures strung together. But look more closely. In a well-plotted episodic novel each new adventure leads the characters, particularly the protagonist, to an ultimate climax. Once that climax is reached and resolved, the novel is finished, the adventures are ended. Such a plot line looks like a jagged series of sawtoothed peaks, where each individual peak is slightly higher than the one preceding it, until the climax is attained — the highest peak of all. A graph of a good episodic novel would look something like a profile of the Himalayas, with Mt. Everest at the climax.

It is very helpful to think carefully about the kind of plot you want to develop for your novel. Pull your ideas and your notes together, go over your plot outline, and draw a graph of the plot you have created. Does the graph match your picture of what the novel is all about? Do you want to write a soul-wrenching tragedy, but find you have a smiling, upward-curving plot line? Time to think about where you are heading.

RESEARCH

Just as there are three kinds of lies — lies, damned lies and statistics — there are three kinds of research:

1. Your own life experiences.
2. Experiences you learn about from others who have lived them.
3. Information you get out of books, films, tapes, etc.

Hemingway is the archetype of the first kind of research. His fiction was based very closely on the life he led. He wrote about the things he did and the people he knew. So much so, in fact, that one of his early novels was described as "six characters in search of the author — with a gun."

All right, probably you have not blown up bridges in Spain or battled a giant marlin single-handedly for days on end or even seen a bullfight. Does that mean you should only try to write about the things you have experienced?

Not necessarily. While it is always best to write about what you know from firsthand experience, the science fiction writer Mickey Zucker Reichert suggests, "If you don't know about it, DO it!" She explains that in the course of researching novels she has "climbed to the roofs of buildings, ridden broncos, allowed martial artists to use me as a punching bag, and driven a Porsche a hundred miles an hour through city streets with my lights turned off.''

I can write about swordplay because I was a champion fencer. I try to travel to the places where my fiction will be set; conversely, I find settings for stories in the places that I have been.

I have never been in space, but when I decided to write a technothriller set on a space station I went to someone who knows the territory, astronaut Bill Pogue, who lived aboard *Skylab* for eighty-four weightless days in 1973-74. He and I co-authored *The Trikon Deception*, with Bill's firsthand experience making the novel very realistic and convincing.

Research should not be confined to places and things, however. Research should include people. More than the backgrounds and settings and mechanical props, it is the people who make novels vivid and enthralling. Draw your characters from the people you know. Learn their passions, their conflicts, their hopes and terrors. People are what fiction is all about, and that kind of experience happens to you every day. Be an observer, a listener. Go beyond noting what people do; ask yourself why a person behaves the way he does, then figure out the answer.

Never worry that the people around you will recognize themselves in your fiction. Unless you work very hard to draw an exact likeness, no one will see herself in your pages. The characters of your story will be composites, based partly on this person, partly on someone else and partly, inevitably, on yourself.

What you have not personally experienced, other people have. If you need to know what it is like to fly a jet fighter in combat, find someone who has done that. The people around you have their own life experiences, which you can tap into. If your novel demands that you must know what it is like to dive for pearls in a tropical lagoon, find someone who has done that. You may have to work your way through many people, even travel to find the person you want. But, short of diving for pearls yourself, learning about the experience from someone who has done it will bring life and vividness to your novel.

In my novel *Mars*, the protagonist is an American geologist who is half Navaho. I knew much about rocketry, astronautics and the political aspects of our space program, but not much about the Navahos, except from visits I had made over the years to New Mexico and Arizona. Before I put the first word of the novel on paper, I went to live in the Santa Fe area and soaked up as much of the feeling of the place and the people as I could. Later, I had to find the Navaho word for Mars. I tracked down one expert after another; none of them knew. Finally, an assistant to the president of the Navaho nation, who happened to be an astronomer, told me that there is no proper name for the planet Mars in the Navaho language. They simply call it "Big Star."

I could have avoided the problem by writing around it and ignoring the Navaho name for Mars. But the novel needed that touch, and I was glad I got my answer, surprising as it was.

Most of the time when someone hears the word *research*, they picture sitting in a library, poring over dusty old tomes of arcane lore. Yes, a good deal of research is just like that. Recently, I needed to find the speeches of the ancient Athenian demagogue, Demosthenes. A couple of lines in the novel I was writing required library research that took several weeks.

But the information you get from books or other research sources should not be limited to seeking answers to specific questions. Do you want to write about ancient Athens? Then steep yourself in everything you can find about the old city. You do not have to travel to modern Athens; in some ways that might even be counterproductive, because you would then be seeing the ruins of the ancient city. Instead, gather every scrap of information you can find about ancient Athens: books, paintings, videotapes, novels, the plays of Athens's great dramatists, the speeches of her political leaders — everything that you can find. Drench yourself in the subject until you dream about ancient Athens. Then you can begin to write.

And do not confine your reading to the subject of your novel. Read as widely as you can. Read for enjoyment as well as research. You will be happily surprised at how many fresh ideas come to you while you are not doing research per se. And you will be broadening your understanding of the world, which is the fundamental wellspring from which you draw your novel.

A NOVEL PREPARATION CHECKLIST
To recapitulate the points of this chapter:

   1. All the earlier material on characters, background, conflict

and plot applies just as much to writing the novel as to writing short fiction.

2. The novel's fundamental difference from short fiction is its greater complexity and depth.

3. Generally, a writer earns more money per hour of work by writing novels than by writing short fiction.

4. Keep a desk book that contains, as a minimum, sections on characters, names, background information, lines and phrases, and a chart of character appearances.

5. Plot outlines should guide your work, not strangle it. The plot outline should answer these five basic questions: 1. Who are the novel's protagonist and antagonist? 2. Where does the novel begin? 3. What are the complications? 4. What is the climax? 5. What is the resolution?

6. There are three types of research: your life experiences; the experiences of people you meet; and library research.

Chapter Sixteen

The Long Siege: Writing the Novel

There are three rules for writing the novel. Unfortunately, no one knows what they are.

—Somerset Maugham

In the previous chapter I stressed the importance of planning and organization: Think before you write. But don't think too much.

Sooner or later you must plant your buttocks on a chair and begin to write. Writing a novel is a long and often difficult commitment. The greatest enemy a novelist faces is delay. So, although it is necessary to prepare, organize, and plan the long siege of writing the novel, do not let preparation get in the way of writing. Get started. And keep at it.

I know some persons who claim they want to be writers yet have never gotten a word on paper. They talk but do not write. There are others who have been gathering the material for their novels ever since I first met them, ages ago. They have not quite reached the point where they are ready to begin writing. I doubt that they ever will.

Like all writers, my friend Harlan Ellison often runs into people who tell him they want to be writers. Before they can get any farther, Harlan asks, "Wait a minute. Do you want to be a writer or do you want to write?"

A writer writes.

To outsiders it looks like grand fun to be a writer. That is because outsiders never see a writer at work. The only time the general public sees a writer is when the writer is at a social gathering, a party, or signing books or giving a lecture or being interviewed. That part of being a writer truly is grand fun. But no one sees the writer sweating over a scene that simply will not come alive or stuck for the precisely right word that will make the sentence sing or simply pounding away at the keyboard, hour after hour, day after day, laboring constantly — and alone.

Especially when it comes to writing a novel, the writer must be prepared for a long, lonely campaign of grinding, unremitting work. There is no other way to get the job done: You just sit there, as one author put it, open a vein and go to work.

WORK HABITS

Let me tell you a story.

In the late 1970s I helped arrange a science fiction cruise sponsored by the Cunard Line. Cunard asked me to invite half a dozen science fiction writers to give lectures during one of their cruises to the West Indies. We received free passage on the cruise liner in return for a few hours of lecturing.

We were quartered in six adjacent cabins. There we were, six of us with our spouses or significant others, with nothing to do for a whole week except give an occasional lecture and enjoy the cruise.

Not quite. If you had tiptoed down the passageway outside our cabins any morning, you would have heard the tap-tap-tap of portable typewriters pecking away. Except for Isaac Asimov's cabin; Isaac was writing in longhand.

All the successful writers I know write every day. Frederik Pohl, for example, sets himself a goal of four pages a day. That does not sound intimidating, does it? You can produce four pages in an hour or two, I imagine. Yet in half a year you can pile up more than seven hundred pages, at four pages a day.

Ah, you say, it's all well and good for a successful writer to talk. The beginning writer does not have all day to write. There's the small matter of earning a living; that takes a big chunk out of the day, you know.

I certainly do know. When I began writing I did not earn enough from my fiction to buy typewriter ribbons, let alone support myself. And I acquired a wife and two children along the way, as well. I worked as a newspaper reporter, technical editor, educational film script writer, marketing executive for a research laboratory, and editor of national magazines. During my checkered career I lived in Philadelphia, Washington, Baltimore, Boston and New York. My work for the research laboratory took me across the United States. My work for *Omni* magazine, years later, took me around the world.

But I was a writer, first and foremost. I wrote every day that I was home and most days when I was on the road. Every morning I would get up two hours before I needed to for my office job—often before the sun came up—and spent those two early hours writing. Then, and only then, would I start my business day. I remember finishing one novel in the dormitory of a university where I was lecturing, working on a flightweight portable typewriter. The *t* key broke as I started the last page of the novel; it sailed right out of the machine and flew across the room. I doggedly finished that final page anyway, then put in all the *t*'s by hand. The page looked like a cemetery.

Even today, after many years of being a writer full time, the first thing I do every day is write. I wake up, get out of bed, get a cup of coffee from the kitchen, and go to my keyboard. Six days a week, sometimes seven. I keep on writing until I get tired, although no matter how weary I may be I stay at work until at least five pages have been done. They may be terrible. I may tear them up tomorrow. But I make myself sit and work that much each day. The habit of working, of regular hours, of constant application, has paid off not only for me, but for every successful writer I know.

So, here are two simple rules for writers who have other jobs or other obligations that take up their days.

1. Pick a time of the day that will be your writing time. It may be early morning or late night or high noon, whichever works best for you. It may be as little as a single hour, but do not make it less than an hour. Make that hour your time for writing. Every day, at least six days a week.

2. Let nothing interfere with that sacred hour. Nothing. Neither family nor job nor blizzards nor hurricanes nor visiting friends. Nothing whatsoever. Even if you do nothing but scratch your head, unable to get a word out, sit at your writing place for that entire hour. Even if your spouse is packing up and leaving you, even if an ambulance is taking your firstborn to the hospital, stay in there and work. If you are a writer, then the writing comes first and everything else, *everything else*, comes afterward.

As William Faulkner put it, "The writer's only responsibility is to his art. He will be completely ruthless . . . Everything goes by the board: honor, pride, decency, security, happiness, all, to get the book written. If the writer has to rob his mother, he will not hesitate; the *Ode on a Grecian Urn* is worth any number of old ladies."

Sound strong? You bet it is! It has to be, because it is so easy to skip a day, to let things slide, to attend to more "important" matters. After all, you can write again tomorrow, or next week.

I have been there. When I was a newspaper reporter it was almost impossible for me to write fiction, or anything else, at home. I spent most of my working day at a typewriter; the juices were being wrung out of me. But somehow I kept at it, and I eventually changed to another job that did not require so much writing.

It is important to find the time of day (or night) that is best for you to write, especially if you can only squeeze out one hour or so for your writing. Years ago a group of us met every year in Milford, Pennsylvania, for a week-long professional writing workshop. One evening during each week we discussed writing habits. I learned that no two writers worked in the same fashion. Some were morning writers; others wrote only between midnight and dawn. Some had to vacuum the carpet and sharpen all their pencils before they could begin to write. One fellow had to put on a certain pair of pajamas and lie prone on his bed, writing with a particular mechanical pencil on a tablet of yellow legal-sized paper.

But all of them wrote every day or night, no matter what other work they did. They were professional writers despite their other jobs or careers.

Ideally, your writing time should be the time of day when you are at your peak. Each of us has a distinctive biorhythm, with peaks of energy at certain hours and valleys of fatigue between them. But if your most energetic hour is in the early afternoon, yet you must be at work during that time earning your daily bread, you will have to settle for another time and do your best— until you reach the happy day when you can write whenever you want to.

Even then, though, pick a certain time of the day for your writing and work at it every day. Be consistent.

NOVELISTIC TECHNIQUES

There are a few tools of the trade that are more useful in writing novels than short stories. This is so mainly because the novel's length and complexity allow the writer to use more sophisticated techniques. The other side of this coin is that the sheer length and depth of the novel virtually *requires* a more complex structure than the short story can stand.

Remember, everything covered in the earlier chapters about characterization, background, conflict and plot applies equally to the novel as well as to shorter fiction. Here are eight areas, however, where the novel permits—indeed, demands—more complex approaches.

Viewpoint

In short fiction it is usually very dangerous to change the viewpoint. Show the story through one character's eyes and stick to that one character's point of view. But the novel allows much greater latitude. Many novels are written from a third-person viewpoint that is almost godlike, in that the third-person narrator can not only flit from one place to another in the span of a short paragraph, but can also reveal the innermost thoughts of any of the novel's characters.

For example, in my novel *Colony* I used a third-person viewpoint because the novel involved dozens of characters and sprawled across the world, from Arabia to Texas to the moon to a space colony a quarter-million miles from Earth. No single character would be in each of those places, so it would be impossible to use a first-person viewpoint, or even the kind of close and immediate third-person viewpoint that I recommended in chapter three. I had to be able to move swiftly from a scene set in Argentina to a scene set in a base on the Moon, scenes populated by entirely different sets of characters.

But I cheated. Instead of using an omniscient third-person narrator, I picked an individual viewpoint character for each individual scene and showed the scene through that character's eyes (and ears, and all the other senses). I used that same close and immediate third-person viewpoint as given in chapter three, but with different viewpoint characters in different scenes.

Picking a couple of scenes at random:

T. Hunter Garrison sat in his powerchair in a corner of his penthouse suite atop the Garrison Tower in Houston. . . . The top floor of the Tower was Garrison's office, his playground, his home. He seldom left it. He seldom had to. The world came to him.

Hideki Tanaka . . . made a few polite remarks about the beauty of the approaching summer. Garrison let him ramble on . . .

"All right," Garrison said . . . "what about this coup in Argentina? How come we didn't know about it beforehand?"

The following scene features Bahjat, the daughter of a sheik, who is secretly Scheherazade, the revolutionary leader:

Sailing under a cobalt-blue sky dotted with happy puffs of cumulus clouds, Bahjat felt her body relaxing under the warmth of the Mediterranean sun and the languid rhythm of the schooner's rising and dipping as it plowed through the deep sea swells.

But her mind could not relax. . . . The captain, a crafty-eyed, solidly-built Turk with a jewel set into one of his front teeth, had invited Bahjat to share his quarters the first night after they had left Tripoli. She declined. He came to her compartment later that night, calmly unlocking the door, smiling at her in her bunk.

The light over her bunk flicked on and he was staring into the muzzle of an automatic, held rock-steady by this little *houri*. The gun itself made the captain hesitate. But when he saw there was a silencer on it, he turned without a word and left her compartment.

She knows guns, was his first thought. His second was, *Someone is probably offering a reward for her.*

Throughout the 470 printed pages of the novel and its forty-three chapters, each scene is shown through the eyes of an individual character. I did not pick viewpoint characters at random, however. There were half a dozen major characters in the novel, and they served as the viewpoint persons for any scenes in which they appeared. If more than one of these major characters appeared in a single scene, I picked either the protagonist, the antagonist, or the strongest character in the scene to be the viewpoint character.

Notice, however, that the second scene described above shifts in midstream from Bahjat's point of view to the captain's. He is a very minor character and does not appear anywhere else in the novel. But it seemed to me to make a more powerful scene if the captain's attempted seduction of Bahjat were shown from his viewpoint rather than hers. I would never try that in a short story!

It is even possible to shift from a first-person viewpoint to a third-person viewpoint in a novel, although I do not recommend the technique for beginners. Read Harold Robbins's *The Carpetbaggers*, however, to see how a master of his craft gets away with this.

Subplots

Short fiction seldom deals with subplots. In the short story you deal with a limited set of characters and have neither the space nor the time to build complicated wheels within wheels. The novel, though, almost demands subplots—conflicts and interactions that are secondary to the main plot of the novel. It is a rare novel that deals with one single plot strand alone. Subplots add depth, complications and surprises to the novel.

Remember the chart of character appearances mentioned in chapter fifteen? It is a useful tool not only for keeping track of your characters, but for creating subplots. In the course of plotting the novel, before you begin to write, you may include one or more subplots. Then, as you write the novel, by checking which characters appear in which chapters, you can generate additional subplots. This is called *compounding*.

In *Colony*, which had a cast of dozens of important characters, I found by checking my chart (which I kept on a large chalkboard) that some of those characters never met each other in the original draft, even though they may have been geographically close to one another. I began to write scenes in which these characters did meet, interact, conflict. The subplots generated by this compounding made the final novel richer, stronger and more interesting.

A word of caution, however. Do not go overboard on subplots. Make certain that your subplots are not so numerous that the reader becomes confused or, worse, bored with seemingly endless complications. Remember that the operative word for subplots is *sub*. These minor conflicts should support and complement the novel's main plot, not compete with it or drown it out altogether.

At the conclusion of your novel the subplots must be resolved, just as the major plot is. Do not leave your readers wondering whether Maxine accepted Max's proposal, or whatever happened to the protagonist's best friend, whom we last saw holding the ladder that our hero used to rescue the heroine from the burning castle.

Maintaining Tension

Think of your novel as an Olympic athlete. An athlete must exercise constantly or run the risk of getting weak and flabby. A novel must crackle with tension on every page or it becomes weak and uninteresting. Yet it is difficult to maintain hard-wired tension throughout the length of a novel.

The best way to keep the story taut is to keep adding links to that chain of promises. Start the novel with a set of problems and never solve one of those problems until you have generated a couple more. The search for the answers will keep the reader turning pages, keep the novel taut and suspenseful.

Since the novel usually has a larger cast of characters than shorter fiction, you can use each new character you introduce as a source of new problems, new tensions. Even in a novel with a limited set of characters, such as F. Scott Fitzgerald's *The Great Gatsby*, each character brings new tensions to the story. Read *Gatsby* and pay particular attention to how Fitzgerald builds the tension with only a handful of characters.

Transitions

Suppose in your novel, scene A ends with your protagonist angrily storming out of his house and scene B begins with him entering the office of an old friend in a city several hundred miles away. You do not want to spend a few pages describing how he got from A to B; that is not essential to the story and would only bog the reader down in boring details.

You could write:

Still trembling with anger even after his five-hour drive, Joe opened the door to Barbara's office and saw her smiling at him from behind her desk.

That sentence is a transition. It telescopes the five-hour interval between the two scenes into a few words. It connects the two scenes by referring to Joe as "still trembling with anger" from his quarrel at home as he "opened the door to Barbara's office," the action that begins the next scene.

Transitions can be a scene, a paragraph, even a single sentence. They are bridges that move the reader smoothly from one scene to the next, even though the two scenes may be separated by many years or many miles. Like a good bridge, a good transition is firmly anchored at each end and strong enough to carry the reader from scene A to scene B.

How do you get from the afternoon of your protagonist's sixteenth birthday to the moment ten years later when she decides to become a neurosurgeon, without describing the intervening ten years? You need a transition.

Try to write a transition in as few words as possible that takes your reader from the protagonist's sixteenth birthday to her fateful decision. Build it like a bridge. Your transition should mention the birthday, the fact that ten years have elapsed, and the fact that the protagonist has decided to make neurosurgery her career.

Remember the scene in *Colony* where the Turkish sea captain tries to seduce Bahjat? I made the transition from Bahjat's viewpoint to the captain's with this sentence:

The light over her bunk flicked on and he was staring into the muzzle of an automatic, held rock-steady by this little *houri*.

Did you notice, when you first read that scene, that this sentence was a transition? I hope not. Like a good butler, transitions should not draw attention to themselves.

Transitions are just as necessary in short fiction as in novels, but because novels contain so many more scenes than shorter fiction, transitions are of special importance to the novelist.

"Meanwhile, back at the ranch . . ." is a transition so familiar that it has become something of a joke. Actually, that transition was invented by Homer, in the *Odyssey*, when his narrative switched back and forth from Odysseus' journeys to his wife's travails back at their home in Ithaca. Many parts of the *Odyssey* begin with the Homeric equivalent of, "Meanwhile, back in Ithaca . . ."

Pay attention to your transitions. Like an architect designing a bridge across a chasm, work hard to make your transitions as strong yet as graceful as possible. Good transitions carry the reader from one place or time to another without a bump or a rattle. Remember, your intention is to keep your reader reading. The shift from one scene to the next is a dangerous place, where the reader may decide to put your book down and go fix a sandwich. Get the reader into that next scene as quickly and effortlessly as possible.

In my novel *Mars*, I needed to show some of the political background that led up to the first human mission there. In particular, I had to introduce the reader to a Brazilian scientist, Dr. Alberto Brumado, who had worked for thirty years to convince the world's governments to send human explorers to the red planet. I inserted three-and-a-half pages of background and history into a scene set in Rio de Janeiro, where Brumado is watching the huge celebration going on in the streets as the populace of the city watches on television the first explorers setting foot on Mars. I describe Brumado physically, then make the transition from here-and-now to the past with this short paragraph:

> If the governments of the world's industrial nations were the brain directing the Mars Project and the multinational corporations were the muscle, then Alberto Brumado was the heart of the mission to explore Mars. No, more still: Brumado was its soul.

The next three-and-a-half pages tell how Brumado worked and schemed for thirty years to get a Mars expedition underway. Then the scene returns to Rio and the day of the first Mars landing with this transition:

> Too old to fly into space himself, Brumado instead watched his daughter board the spacecraft that would take her to Mars.
>
> Now he had watched her step out onto the surface of

that distant world, while the crowd outside chanted their name.

Chapter Endings

Transitions are different from chapter endings, although both have the same ultimate function: to prevent the reader from putting the book down. Transitions should be smooth and as invisible as possible. The reader should not realize the scene has been changed until well into the new scene.

Chapter endings, on the other hand, can often be cliff-hangers. Literally. Break the action at a high point and start the next chapter. Force the reader to turn the page and get into the new chapter to find out what happens next.

Back when we were teenagers, a dear friend of mine got a job with a local television station splicing commercials into the ancient movies they showed late at night. Once he cut a western in the middle of a barroom brawl, just as the hero was throwing a haymaker at the villain. After a string of commercials, the western came on the screen again and *bam!* the bad guy was knocked for a loop. That's the way to end one chapter and start a new one.

Time and Flashbacks

Time in fiction is not the same as time in real life. A novel may encompass the entire life of a character or more. Some of James Michener's novels, for example, span not merely many human generations but geologic ages, as well. It is obviously neither necessary nor desirable for the writer to record every moment of the entire time span encompassed by the novel.

As we saw in the previous section, you can move from one time to another with transitions. They must be carefully thought out and even more carefully written, so that the reader is not confused by the shift in time.

There are three novels that you should read with particular attention to the way their authors move the stories through jumps in time: Kurt Vonnegut's *Slaughterhouse Five*, Joseph Heller's *Catch 22*, and Joseph Conrad's *Lord Jim*. Conrad's novel, published in 1900, still sets the standard for jumping back and forth in time without the slightest misstep. Read it and see what a master of the craft can accomplish.

In *Mars*, I wanted to start the novel with the moment the first spacecraft of explorers touches down on the red planet's surface. I felt this was necessary to grab the reader's attention. That meant that I had to make the "now" of the novel the days and nights that the exploring team spends on Mars. Everything that happened earlier, their training, the political machinations of picking the crew, the characters' younger years—all that had to be shown in flashbacks.

To make certain that these flashbacks were clearly separated from the ongoing action of the main narrative (the novel's now), I placed the flashbacks in separate chapters and labeled them differently from the chapters describing their exploration of Mars.

Flashbacks are often used to show a particular incident that illuminates a character's motivations. In *Mars*, for example, I went as far back as the protagonist's childhood visits to his Navaho grandfather.

It is important that the flashbacks you use do not stop the flow of the main story. Flashbacks should support your story, not interrupt it. Think of them as clues you offer to the reader, clues to help the reader understand who your characters truly are and why they are behaving the way they do. Get back to the main story promptly.

Dialogue

There are two things to keep in mind about writing dialogue: Keep it short and keep it natural. But natural is not what you might at first think it to be.

Listen to the way people speak. Tape record normal, everyday conversations. When you listen to the playback you will find that normal conversation is filled with meaningless blather.

"Er, I was talking to, you know, the kid with the weird, uh, haircut, and he sort of—oh, what's his name? Kenny? Yeah, Kenny. I think that's his name. Well, anyway, he tells me . . ."

If you tried to put that kind of natural dialogue into a novel, no one would have the patience to read past page 3.

On the other hand, it will not do to make your dialogue so precise and functional that it sounds stilted.

"I was speaking with Kenneth. His haircut is quite unusual. He told me that. . . ."

The trick of writing dialogue is to make it look natural, but without all the hesitations and circumlocutions and other wasted words that each of us uses in our everyday speech. Ernest Hemingway was a master of naturalistic dialogue. It looks right on the page; it sounds in our inner ear like the way people actually do talk. But read a couple of pages of Hemingway's dialogue aloud and you realize that no one actually speaks that way. It looks right on the page, yes. But it took all of Hemingway's genius to fool you into thinking that the characters would actually speak that way.

Listen to the way people speak, then get the flavor of it on your pages. The flavor. Do not reproduce conversations word for word. Get the flavor, not the substance.

The same thing applies to using accents or the broken English of foreigners. Mark Twain was a stickler for reproducing the various accents of the people who lived along the Mississippi in his youth. In *Huckleberry Finn* he makes it a point of author's pride to get those accents down accurately. But the modern writer should use more suggestion than reproduction.

If you have an Italian character say, "I'ma gonna break-a ever' bone inna hissa body," it looks difficult to read and sounds to the reader's inner ear suspiciously like a caricature, even if it is a faithful reproduction of that character's heavy accent. Better to write, "I'ma gonna break every bone in his body." Enough of the accent comes through to get the flavor. Do not drown the reader in broken English.

And keep the dialogues short. Whenever a character speaks more than a few lines at a time you stop having dialogue, you have a lecture instead.

Run your eye down the right margin of a page of dialogue. It should be very ragged and uneven. There should not be large blocks of type. Veteran film writers can cast their eyes over a script and decide if it will work well on camera merely by the amount of white space on the page. Too much type means lectures, not dialogue.

Remember the acronym KISS: Keep It Short, Sweetheart.

Minor Characters

Novels usually have a larger cast of characters than short fiction. How much is it necessary for the reader to know about the minor characters? How much should you tell about a minor character's background?

If the character is truly minor, no background is really needed. Just show the character in action and do not worry about her motivation. But there is a gray area where a minor character may be pivotal to your plot, and it is important for the reader to understand where this person is coming from. In that case, some of the character's background should be sketched in.

Remember, it is always better to show than to tell. By showing the character in action you may be able to reveal as much of his background as you need to. If you feel it is absolutely imperative to stop the flow of the story and give a few pages of background information about the character, well, go ahead and do it. But when you rewrite the novel, you may be surprised to find out that although *you* needed to know that background information, the reader can do very well without it.

BAD DAYS

Every writer has bad days when nothing seems to go right, when you can't get the words on paper, and even those few you do manage to squeeze out are dull and stupid.

Sometimes the bad days just keep on coming, and the writer falls victim to "writer's block": an inability to write anything at all. Some writers are blocked for years; they do not produce a readable word. Frankly, I have never seen anyone with writer's block who did not have some other way to pay for the groceries. Perhaps a job, perhaps a working spouse, perhaps a generous friend. My suspicion is that if you locked the blocked writer in a jail cell without hope of getting out until some reasonably good fiction was produced, the blockage would evaporate soon enough.

But perhaps I am too harsh.

All writers have bad days. Listen to Joseph Conrad: "I sit down religiously every morning. I sit down for eight hours a day — and the sitting down is all. In the course of that working day of eight hours I write three sentences which I erase before leaving the table in despair. . . . Sometimes it takes all my resolution and power of self-control to refrain from butting my head against the wall."

There are those days when nothing seems to be coming

through. You sit there and nothing is happening. The blank page, or blank screen, stares at you and you stare back. What to do?

To quote Douglas Adams, "Don't panic."

The problem may be inside you. Perhaps you are coming down with a cold, or you had an argument with your loved one, or a manuscript of yours just returned, rejected again. It is tough to sit down and write creatively when you are feeling ill or miserable. Yet, as Humphrey Bogart put it, a professional is a guy who gets the job done whether he feels like it or not.

Do not abandon ship. No matter how awful you feel, sit down at your writing desk and try to scratch out a few words. Make the effort. You may be happily surprised to see a decent sentence take shape. Maybe a complete paragraph. Perhaps even a whole page.

Starting is the toughest part of it. Inertia is a very real condition, and getting started when you would rather be in bed or at the beach or anywhere except there at your desk takes guts. I am going to let you in on a secret: Only the writers with guts succeed. Have you ever wondered why writers of mediocre talent get published while greater talents do not? The answer is guts. Drive. Perseverance. Talent is not enough. You must have the drive to overcome all obstacles, including your own inertia.

Judith Krantz put it this way: "To be successful you must have talent joined with the willingness, the eagerness, to work like a dog. I write seven days a week from ten until four, and I begrudge every minute I have to spend on the phone or away from my typewriter."

Perhaps, though, the problem is not inside you. It may be in the novel. You may have somehow gotten off the track and are bogged down so badly that you do not know what to do. There is no scarier feeling than the realization that you have no idea what your characters are going to do next.

This is where your earlier planning can come to your rescue. Like a detective, you must find out why the novel has gone off-beam, and just where it started to wander down the wrong trail. Check your outline. Cast an analytical eye on your chart of character appearances. Read your notes.

You will find that one of two things has happened. Either you have lost track of the story you started to tell, or your characters are trying to make you see that you are forcing them to do things they do not want to do.

Do not despair. This is a decisive moment. Are you going to stick to your original plot or allow your characters to move in the direction they want to go? There is no way that I can give you an answer. The answer has got to come out of you. You have invested a great deal of time and effort in developing these characters and the plot of your novel. Which is more important? Only you can decide.

You may find that you drifted away from your original outline, and by going back a bit and sticking closer to the original plot the story comes alive again and all is well. Or you may decide to chuck the outline and follow where the characters are leading. It may seem strange to allow fictitious personalities to direct your writing, but remember these personalities are creatures of your subconscious mind. You created them. When they tell you they want to go one way while your plot insists they go another, you are arguing within yourself, and that is why you find it difficult to write. Restore your inner harmony and the words will flow again.

Recognize that every novelist comes to a low point somewhere along the line in every novel. I call it the "slough of despond." For some reason, the whole world seems "weary, stale, flat and unprofitable." When you have been working on the same novel for many months and the end is still nowhere in sight, you can become mentally fatigued and the whole story begins to seem wearisome and dull to you.

The only advice I can offer for the slough of despond is to tough it out. As long as you can keep getting the words down, as long as the novel is moving along, keep at it. Sooner than you think, the end will come and you will be finished. Then you can begin the rewrite, which is much easier and more of a joy.

There are a couple of little tricks that can help you over bad days, or even prevent them from happening in the first place.

One is to stop your day's work before you are totally drained of ideas. Stop while you still know what the next sentence will be. Some writers even stop in the middle of a sentence. Then the next day they sit down, finish the sentence, and they are off and writing without that dreaded starting inertia bogging them down. One of the benefits of that technique is that your subconscious mind will be working on that unfinished sentence during the time you are not writing. You may be happily surprised to find, once you sit down to your work again, that your subconscious mind has plunged onward far beyond that one sentence.

Another trick is to just start typing. Anything, even nonsense or gibberish. Some writers have found this useful. The theory is that a professional writer cannot write gibberish for very long. Before you type three or four lines you will be writing decent sentences. You will be continuing your novel by the end of the page.

That is the theory. I know one writer who found himself unable to get any decent work out, but he swore to himself that he would sit at his desk every morning and force himself to write at least one page, even if it was gibberish. He found himself typing, "Only fifteen more lines to the end of the page. Only fourteen more lines. . . ." And so on until he finished the page and ran away to play.

Don't let that happen to you!

REWRITING

First drafts are a chore. But your job is not finished with the end of the first draft. In fact, the real work is just beginning. You know who your characters are and what they have done. Now you can begin to polish, rearrange, remove unnecessary lines or even whole scenes, insert new material where it is needed, and just generally spiff up the novel until it sparkles in the sunlight.

Rewriting is hard work, of course, but a different kind of work from writing the original draft. Ernest Hemingway advised, "Don't get discouraged because there's a lot of mechanical work to writing. . . . I rewrote the first part of *A Farewell to Arms* at least fifty times. . . . The first draft of anything is shit." Strongly put, but the point is valid: Any good piece of fiction is worth all the labor it takes to rewrite it until it is as good as you can make it.

To rewrite effectively you need to see the novel in its entirety with fresh eyes. It is best to get away from it for a while, a month or more if you can, and then read it through from beginning to end. You will be surprised at how good it is. Nowhere near as bad as you thought when you were halfway through the first draft, struggling against the slough of despond. Still, it could be a lot better.

Learn to be not merely analytical with your own work, but ruthless. There may be a little jewel of a scene imbedded in your novel that does nothing for the story. It's beautiful, but superfluous. Cut it out. Save it for another day, perhaps, but do not leave it in the novel just because you think it is pretty.

I have seldom read the first drafts of friends' novels where the entire first chapter could not be removed. Many writers have the tendency to start their novels with a chapter full of background information that they have to know in order to write the rest of the novel. But the reader does not have to be burdened with such material. Inevitably, that first chapter comes out during the rewriting process, and the novel becomes tighter and faster-paced.

The computer is a great help in rewriting. It allows you to move sentences, paragraphs, whole pages or even chapters from one place in the novel to another with the touch of a few keys. And then you can move it all back to where it was originally, if you do not like the change.

Rewrite with care. Think of yourself as a sculptor. Your first draft has chiseled the rough shape of your statue out of the blank stone. Now you must carve carefully and polish beautifully to make the statue as lifelike as possible.

There is the great temptation to tell yourself that the novel is finished at last and to send it off to market. But wait, think, read it again carefully. Perhaps a bit more polish will make the difference between a rejection and a sale. Do not be in such a rush to send the novel off. I know you have been working on it for a long, long time, and you want to get it out into the world. But always remember that you want to send your best work to an editor, nothing less. Keep working on the novel until you can honestly say that you cannot make it any better than it is now.

My novel *Millennium* has a long and torturous history. I worked on it, off and on, for fully twenty-five years. And it was not until the very last moment that I finally wrote its last paragraph. For twenty-five years I struggled with various drafts of that novel, until the day when that ultimate paragraph came to me. Then I knew it was finished. Then I sent it to my publisher.

You do not have to work on your novel for twenty-five years!

(Indeed, the next novel I wrote, *The Starcrossed*, a comedy, took only a few months.) But the time you spend polishing your novel will pay great dividends, if you rewrite with care. And love.

A NOVEL-WRITING CHECKLIST

1. The greatest enemy a novelist faces is delay.

2. Write every day, preferably at the same time of the day, and let nothing interfere with your writing time.

3. There are eight tools that are important to the novelist over and above the techniques discussed for short fiction: viewpoint changes, subplots, maintaining tension, transitions, chapter endings, time and flashbacks, dialogue, and handling minor characters.

4. Every novelist has bad days. Only intense dedication and perseverance can overcome the inertia that prevents you from writing.

5. Every novelist falls into the slough of despond somewhere along the long road to the finished novel. Keep working!

6. Rewriting is as important as the original writing was. Think of yourself as a sculptor, polishing your statue until it shines in the sun.

Chapter Seventeen

Into the Cold, Cruel World: Marketing Your Fiction

No man but a blockhead ever wrote except for money.
    — Samuel Johnson

I f you wish to be a writer," said the Stoic philosopher Epictetus, "write."

If you wish to be a professional writer, you must send your work to the marketplace.

There are those who write for themselves and never even try to sell their work. There are those who show their stories to a select group of friends or to writers' workshops, but never send the stories to market. If you are writing merely to satisfy your own ego, I suppose that's all right. But most of us write to *sell*, and believe me, when an editor sends you a check for what you have written, that is the biggest ego-boost imaginable.

FAMILY, FRIENDS AND WORKSHOPS

While selling a story or a novel is tremendously satisfying, gratifying, pleasurable and all that, having a manuscript bounced back to you, rejected, makes you feel as if an anvil has been dropped on your head from a considerable height. I have had my share of story rejections, and they always hurt.

You may be tempted to try out your story on family or friends before taking that big step of mailing it to some publisher. You may even sign up for a writers' workshop to have your story critiqued by professionals.

I feel that it is worse than useless to show your manuscript to family or friends, unless they happen to be professional writers or editors. What good can they do for you? They will probably tell you they like your story. Wonderful. Does that mean they have spotted its weaknesses but think it is strong enough to be published despite its flaws? No, it simply means they want you to feel good. Or, worse yet, they tell you they don't like the story. You are crushed. Why don't they like it? They do not know . . . it just didn't come across to them. That's like a physician telling you that you have two weeks left to live but he doesn't quite know what is wrong with you.

Workshops are fine if they are run by professionals and your manuscript is reviewed by professionals. Otherwise, workshops are a waste of time. You want advice that will help you, not the opinions of more amateurs. Beware especially of local workshops created by the neighborhood "wannabe" writers. Their opinions are not much better than your mother's, and they also have the nasty problem of ego. Chances are they will tear down your story to boost their own morale.

The Milford Science Fiction Writers' Workshop (of blessed memory) was the best experience I have ever had as a writer. Originally organized by Damon Knight, Judith Merrill and James Blish, the workshop met in Milford, Pennsylvania, most years. It was called a science fiction writers' workshop because the organizers recruited members by looking for new names in the science fiction magazines. But any and all types of fiction were welcome at Milford.

For one solid week of the year we talked, ate, slept, breathed nothing but writing. Only published writers were invited, and the group was kept to between twenty and thirty writers each year. There were regulars who came year after year, but there were always newcomers to keep the conference from getting stale and repetitive.

To attend the conference you had to bring a manuscript that had not yet been published; preferably one that was giving you trouble. In the mornings we read each other's manuscripts. In the afternoons three or four stories were critiqued by the group. It was the best learning experience I ever had, and it established friendships that have endured through the years.

If you can find a workshop that offers professional review of your work, fine. Otherwise, advice from friends, family and local wannabe writers will probably do nothing more than befuddle or demoralize you.

DEALING WITH REMOTE EDITORS

There is no way to become a published writer except to send your manuscript to an editor at a publishing house.

It is like sending your first-born infant out onto the river in a leaky basket. You have this terrible feeling that you will never see your creation again, yet at the same time you have the desperate hope that this kid might turn out to be another Moses.

What actually happens is that your manuscript arrives at an editor's office, where it is put into the slushpile of unsolicited manuscripts. It will be read eventually by a first reader, a junior editor on the staff. However, at some book publishers, unsolicited manuscripts are not read at all! I will tell you how to deal with that problem in a moment.

The editor who reads your manuscript has never met you. You know nothing about this editor, not even if it is a man or a woman. The only link between the two of you is your manuscript. You cannot persuade, cajole, flatter or bribe this unknown editor. Your story will sell or be rejected based solely on what you have written.

Almost invariably, manuscripts sent in by unknown authors are read (if at all) by the most junior editor on the staff. This has always seemed stupid to me. The most important job an editor has is to find new talent, yet virtually every publishing house gives the job of discovering new talent to the least experienced person in the office. That is like ordering the newest recruit to lead the platoon through the jungle while the experienced officers ensconce themselves in a posh restaurant.

The only exceptions that I know of are in a few science fiction magazines, where the search for new talent is intense, and the editorial staffs are so small that there is hardly any difference between the first reader and the editor-in-chief. When I was a magazine editor I personally read all the incoming manuscripts, especially the slushpile. I discovered quite a few new stars that way, including Spider Robinson, Orson Scott Card, Vonda N. McIntyre, George R.R. Martin, Joe Haldeman and several others.

In general, though, your manuscript will be read by an inexperienced stranger. That does not mean that the junior editor who first takes up your story lacks knowledge or enthusiasm, merely that the first reader in most publishing houses is the low person on the totem pole, without the experience or the clout to convince the more senior editors to take a gamble on something really new and different.

That is why it is so vitally important that you learn how to market your fiction.

MARKET RESEARCH

There is an old story about a man who wanted to open a supermarket in a certain neighborhood, so he took a job as a garbage collector first. After several months of collecting the neighborhood garbage, he knew exactly what the people bought. When he opened his supermarket he stocked it with the items his customers preferred and was an immediate success.

That is market research. Find out what the customers want and give it to them.

You can do market research for your fiction, whether you are writing short stories or novels. I will discuss the market research for novels first and for short stories afterward.

There are two ways to do market research for a novel. First, you can be like our garbage-collecting entrepreneur: Find out what the market wants and then give it to them. If novels about romance in exotic settings are hot, you sit down and write a romantic novel set in Thailand.

There are a couple of problems with that approach, though. First, by the time you finish your novel the topic may no longer be so hot. The marketplace may be flooded with romances set in Thailand. Second, you run the risk of doing less than your creative best if you set yourself the task of writing a particular kind of novel. Writers can turn into hacks by pounding out quickie works to satisfy an existing market.

There is an alternative. Write the novel you want to write, then do the market research that will tell you which publisher is apt to buy it.

Realize that publishers nowadays think in terms of categories. They publish very little general fiction, but instead establish lines for various categories such as mysteries, historical novels, science fiction, romance, etc. Book publishers hire editors to direct the different lines they publish. Not every type of novel will be bought by every reader, obviously. Women who read gothics seldom buy science fiction. Science fiction readers tend to keep away from romance novels. Mystery fans buy mystery novels, and trying to interest them in bodice-ripping historical novels is usually a waste of effort.

When an editor first looks at a new manuscript he automatically asks himself, "What category does this novel fit into?" Is it a romance, a mystery, western, science fiction, technothriller, horror—what? A novel that is simply good general fiction, with no particular category, will have a much more difficult time finding a publisher. *Literature* is something that publishers often give speeches about, but they seldom publish it. They want novels in categories that they can easily identify. They want products that they can put through their sales system and stock on bookstore shelves under an existing category.

Look around your local bookstores and see how the shelves are organized. New releases are up front, but the books only stay there for a week or so. Then they go to the category shelves, westerns or romances or mysteries or what-have-you. Of course, there is a set of shelves for best-sellers. That is the best place to be, but only a chosen few get there. Isaac Asimov turned out more than two hundred books over forty years before he hit the best-seller lists.

To market your novel you must do what the publishers do. Ask yourself what category your novel fits into. Is it a horror story? A science fiction tale? A romantic adventure? A hard-boiled detective mystery?

Once you have identified your novel's category, browse through the bookshops and take notes about which publishers are putting out that kind of book. You will notice that Publisher A does a lot of mysteries while Publisher B seems to specialize in science fiction and horror. You may further note that there are subdivisions within some categories. Mysteries can range from English drawing-room puzzle stories to hard-edged, realistic police procedurals, for example. SF covers a tremendous span, from the robots and spaceships of true science fiction to the wizards and swordsmen of heroic fantasy.

Once you have identified the category that best fits your novel and the publishers who put out that kind of book, repair to the local library and look up *Literary Market Place, Novel and Short Story Writer's Market,* or one of the other numerous guides to marketing your fiction. These guides list the book and magazine publishers in the United States, and give names and titles of their staffs. From them you can get the address of your chosen publisher and the name of the editor to whom you should write.

Do not send your manuscript. Not yet. Write that editor a letter. This is called a query letter. Its purpose is to ask the editor if she is willing to read your novel. To get the editor to say yes, you should include pertinent information about your novel and yourself. If you have writing credits, tell the editor what they are. Make the letter brief, succinct, professional. Enclose the first chapter or two of your novel and a synopsis of the remainder. Include a stamped, self-addressed envelope large enough to hold the portion of the manuscript you have enclosed.

Now look at this situation from the editor's point of view. Here she is, overworked and underpaid, buried alive under manuscripts and query letters. She spends her days (and probably a good many of her nights) reading manuscripts. Why should she want to read yours?

Your letter must intrigue her enough to make her read your sample chapters. Those chapters must be good enough to make her want to read the rest of the manuscript. Your synopsis must convince her that you have indeed finished the novel, and that it is done well.

Thus, your letter must be a first-rate piece of writing. It is a sales document, a bit of persuasion written for a person you have never met. Do not try to make it cute or overly clever. Editors have seen thousands of letters written in colored ink or decorated with little drawings. Do not use fancy computerized typefaces. Make your letter clear, direct, and as convincing as you can. Make it easy to read. Make it professional.

MARKETING SHORT FICTION

Short fiction is generally published in magazines. While there are occasional anthologies of new fiction published, usually these are open only to writers specifically invited by the editor to contribute. Your short fiction may eventually be reprinted in an anthology, but your first market will undoubtedly be the magazine market.

Every magazine has its own special audience. The editor of a successful magazine knows what that audience wants to read, and continually produces it. Occasionally, the editor will try to lead the audience to newer and, one hopes, better things. But if the editor strays too far from the audience's preferences, the audience stops reading the magazine. And the editor starts looking for a new job.

Because magazines are so specialized, it is probably a good idea to have a particular magazine—or at least a particular type of magazine—in mind before you begin to write a piece of short fiction. Be sure that you are familiar with the style and format of the stories that the magazine publishes. As the salesmen say in Meredith Willson's musical comedy *The Music Man*, "You've got to know the territory." To a writer, this means being thoroughly familiar with the audience you are trying to reach.

There is no sense in sending a hard-core science fiction story to *The New Yorker*, just as it's futile to send an enigmatic tale of frustration and despair to *Analog*, the bastion of upbeat hard-core science fiction. There is no sense in sending a forty-thousand-word manuscript to *Omni*, a magazine that seldom publishes more than seven thousand words of fiction per issue. Nor is there any sense in sending a story that attacks hotel chains and tourism to a magazine that depends on hotel and airline advertising.

It does not matter how well your story is written. These realities of the marketplace have nothing to do with the quality of the writing. No editor will buy a story that does not fit the audience, quality notwithstanding. Before you send an editor a manuscript, make certain that you understand what that editor can buy. Read the magazine before you write for it. I have always found that if I do not enjoy reading the magazine, I will not be able to sell a story to that audience, no matter how earnestly I try.

Do not delude yourself into thinking that although the editor has never before published a science fiction story, he will publish your science fiction story because it is so beautifully done. He won't. It's about as likely as an automobile salesman giving you a car free because he likes your face.

Understand the audience. Remember that the editor buys what the editor feels will be right for that audience, no matter what his individual feelings may be. When I was a magazine editor I had to reject many a lovely story, reluctantly, because it was not right for the audience I worked for.

If you are in doubt about an editor's requirements, by all

means write a query letter. Editors are glad to send out information about their requirements. It saves them the trouble of reading stories that have no chance of making it in their market.

DO YOU NEED AN AGENT?

Paranoia is the occupational disease of writers, especially when they are sending manuscripts out to market, and they are rejected time and again. You get to thinking that the editors could not possibly be reading your work; they are sending it back without even looking at the marvels you have created.

If only you had an agent! Manuscripts sent to a publisher by an agent are treated differently than unsolicited manuscripts. They do not go onto the slushpile; agented manuscripts get more and quicker and better attention than manuscripts sent in by unknown writers.

That is entirely true.

Should you, then, try to get an agent to represent you, rather than send your manuscripts to market yourself?

No. You should not. It would be a waste of time. Agents almost never represent writers who have not yet been published. It is the literary equivalent of Catch 22: You need an agent to get published, but most agents will not take on an unpublished writer.

Actually, you do not need an agent at the very outset of your writing career. In fact, you should be very wary of an agent who offers to represent you before you have published anything.

My wife is a very successful literary agent, so what I am about to tell you comes from my own experience as a writer and former editor, and from close observation of her work as an agent.

First, no agent likes to handle short stories. The work involved in selling a short story to an editor is not much less than the work of selling a novel, and the pay is much less. Remember, the agent only gets 10 to 15 percent of what you earn. Reputable agents get no other income, only a percentage of what they sell for you. That means that short fiction is simply not worth their time.

Besides, you can market your short fiction almost as effectively as an agent can, if you have been slanting your stories to particular magazines. If you have done the marketing research discussed earlier in this chapter, you know the magazines you are aiming for, their audiences and their editors, as well as an agent would. Especially in the science fiction field, where there are fewer than a dozen professional magazines published, it is just as easy for you to keep tabs on which magazine is right for you as it would be for an agent to do so.

Yes, an agent may know the editors personally, but that is not as big a help as you may think. A personal friendship is not going to sell a poor story or a story that is not aimed squarely at the magazine's audience.

An agent can be very helpful in selling your novel: first, by actually getting an editor to read and buy the novel; then in negotiating the contract that the publisher offers you.

Since it is extremely rare for an agent to agree to represent an unpublished writer, you are going to have to make that first sale for yourself. It seems impossible, but just about every writer you have ever read has done it. You have to climb that first mountain alone. Then it gets easier.

Many writers break into print by writing short stories or nonfiction articles for magazines. Then you have writing credits that will help convince an agent to take you seriously. You can also market your own novel, using the market research techniques outlined earlier in this chapter. If and when an editor tells you that she wants to buy your novel, you can and should look for an agent who can help you negotiate the best possible terms for your book contract.

How do you find a good agent? Again, *Literary Market Place* or *Guide to Literary Agents and Art/Photo Reps* list the top agents in the business. Check them out. Write to them. Ask them who they represent. Ask them if they will take on a new, untried client—who has a book contract on her desk. Tell them your previous writing credits. Do not send your novel or any other manuscripts. If an agent is interested in representing you, he will ask to read the novel that the publisher wants to buy.

Not only does a good agent help you to sell your novels, he also sells subsidiary rights, such as overseas publication in foreign languages, audio tape rights, electronic, motion picture and television rights. Usually the book's publisher wants to take those rights and make those sales, giving the writer a percentage of the income. Your agent will strive to keep those rights for you, so that you can control such sales and keep the earnings for yourself. Subsidiary rights can be an important source of additional income, a source that you might never get without the help of a good agent.

The relationship between an author and agent is as close as marriage, and sometimes as stormy. It can be a very emotional relationship even if you have never met your agent face-to-face, but have only corresponded with her or talked on the telephone. Your agent has your career in her hands, after all. Every time your agent hiccups you break out in a sweat. Sometimes you find that the relationship is not working; you are unhappy with your agent. Just as in a marriage, first you try to identify the problem and fix it. But if, after a decent attempt to patch things up, you are still unhappy, then it is time to say farewell and go looking for another agent.

While some agents insist on a written agreement with their writers, most need nothing more than a letter or a handshake. Beware of contracts that bind you to an agent for a fixed length of time and are automatically renewed unless you inform the agent you want to break the agreement. If a simple "me your writer, you my agent" letter will not satisfy the agent, go look for someone else. If the agent does not trust your word, why should you trust his?

The only money your agent should make off you is a percentage of your earnings. If the agent does not sell your work, the agent makes nothing. You should never have to pay a reading fee or anything else to your agent. The money flows from agent to writer, not the other way. The agent may legitimately charge you for extraordinary expenses, such as overseas mailing costs or long-distance telephone calls, but those charges should come out of the money you earn. And even there, beware the agent that totes up every nickel the way a lawyer does.

When agents negotiate a book contract, they include a clause that says, essentially, the publisher will pay any and all monies earned by the book to the agent. You depend on the agent's honesty to pay you, and pay you on time. The publisher sends royalty statements every six months; if those statements do not agree with the checks your agent has been sending you, find out why. If you change agents, the publisher will still send the royalties earned by your book to the "agent of record," the agent who originally negotiated the contract. That is the agent's annuity:

No matter which agent now represents you, the royalties for *that* book go to your old agent, who is entitled to his percentage.

Remember that your agent can only be as tough in negotiations as you allow. If your agent advises you to reject the publisher's offer unless he doubles the size of the advance he is offering, but you are afraid that if you do so the publisher will drop your book back in your lap, you have the right to tell the agent to take the offer regardless of what she wants to do. But realize that you took on this agent to negotiate the best contracts you can get; she ought to know what the traffic will bear much better than you do. After all, it is her business to know. And she is not as emotionally wrapped up in the book as you, the author, are.

I am convinced that one of the greatest benefits an agent gives you is to serve as a buffer between you and the cruel world out there. When your agent writes or phones to tell you that Publisher X has rejected your novel, she will also inform you that she has already sent it to Jane Doe at Publisher Y, whom she knows to like your sort of work. You don't get the full emotional blast of the rejection. And you can scream at your agent about how stupid the editor was who rejected your manuscript. She might even agree with you.

In summary, an agent is invaluable once a publisher has offered to buy your novel. The author-agent relationship is very close, very personal. It is difficult to find a good agent, but once you find the one who is right for you, you are likely to stick with him until death do you part. Still, remember President Reagan's byword: "Trust, but verify." Read your royalty statements carefully.

MANUSCRIPT PREPARATION

Make no mistake about it: The physical appearance of a manuscript is important.

Of course, if you are Danielle Steel or Alexander Solzhenitsyn, any publisher will be glad to take a manuscript of yours no matter what condition it is in. But if you are a new writer, just getting started, you have to make it as easy as possible for an editor to read your work. He has to read it before he can buy it, remember.

When you go out on a date, you don't purposely wear clothes that will annoy your friend or deliberately behave in a slovenly manner, do you? The same commonsense rules apply to making your manuscript look neat, clean and professional.

Look at it from the editor's point of view. She reads manuscripts every day. That is what she does for a living. She reads long ones and short ones. Night and day. Weekends, too, very often. Her eyes are weakening, her stomach is turning sour, her whole body is atrophying from lack of exercise. Imagine how she feels when she gets a manuscript that is handwritten. Or a photocopy that is gray print on grayer paper. Or even a manuscript that's been typed entirely in italic script.

The basic rule of manuscript preparation is, Make the reading as easy as possible. Remember, after the editor buys it, a typesetter must read it with the copyeditor's handwritten instructions on it. If the manuscript is sloppy at the outset, the editor will never pass it on to the copyeditor and typesetter. It would be more trouble than it is worth. There are a hundred other manuscripts waiting to be read. Why bother with one that looks unprofessional and will be difficult to work with?

It would be a wonderful world if the editor could read each manuscript with complete, calm detachment, weighing the merits of each story strictly on their own, with no thought to the lousy lunch he just had, or the phone ringing at his elbow, or the approaching deadline date. Alas, such a Utopia doesn't exist. So make your manuscript as easy to read as possible; it is going to run into plenty of competition, and not merely from other manuscripts, either.

In general, it takes very little extra work to make the manuscript attractive and professional-looking. It must be typed. If you cannot type you should certainly learn how to, especially in this day of word-processing computers. If you have a friend who can type well, fine. But you should learn for yourself. A good carpenter does not go running to a friend for help in driving nails.

Make certain that your typewriter or computer printer is putting black letters on the page, not gray. Use white paper. Fancy paper is a waste of money and harder to read. The typing should be double-spaced, and there should be wide margins on either side and plenty of room at the top and bottom of each page. You should get between 200 to 250 words per page. Three hundred per page should be an outside limit; beyond that the page begins to appear too crowded.

On the first page of the story you should have the story title, your name and address. You might also include your telephone number. For short fiction sent to magazines, you should also include an approximate word count. If you use a computer, of course you can give a precise word count. It is also a good idea to put a cover page over the manuscript and include the word count, title, name and address on that, as well. If you do not use a computer, you can estimate the word count by picking ten or twelve lines at random from the story and averaging the word count in them. Then multiply that averaging by the total number of lines in the story. It is very approximate, but if the editor has any quibbles he will get an accurate word count for himself.

Some writers staple their manuscripts together, often with so many staples that it is difficult to open the pages and read the story. A simple paper clip will do, unless the manuscript is so bulky that you need something stronger. In that case, put strong layers of cardboard on the front and back of the manuscript and wrap the whole thing with a few strong rubber bands. Novel manuscripts should be packed in a box, such as the box your typing paper came in.

Of course you must include return postage and a self-addressed envelope for mailing, in the unhappy event that your story is rejected. Do not expect editors to mail your manuscript back to you out of their own funds.

COVER LETTERS

There is nothing wrong with sending in your manuscript without a covering letter, as long as the manuscript has all the necessary information on it. Most cover letters go unread anyway.

Some short-story writers feel it is necessary to summarize the story in the letter they send atop the manuscript. That is a dangerous thing to do, because a very busy editor (or a very lazy one) might be tempted to scan the summary and not read the story itself. No summary can ever be as deep or strong or good as the story itself.

On the other hand, when I was an editor I saw countless cover letters that were much better written than the stories beneath them! Evidently the writer was relaxed, loose, and speaking with his own true voice when he wrote the letter. But he was Writing (with a capital W) in the manner of a Writer when he did the story. If these newcomers could use the style and grace they show in their cover letters, and forget whatever rules of writing they apply in their stories, they might well become top-flight professionals. They have the talent, but they muffle their own voices when they begin to write fiction.

A FINAL WORD ABOUT EDITORS

When the happy day arrives and your story is bought, you will have to work with not only the wonderful and wise editor who recognized your talent and bought your story, but you will sooner or later encounter a copyeditor.

Most magazines do not have the time or the inclination to send your copyedited manuscript back to you for your comments and/or corrections. Many magazines do send page proofs of your piece, once it has been set in type. Read those proofs carefully, for they will show what the copyeditor has changed in your manuscript.

Changed? My manuscript? As Rostand's Cyrano de Bergerac says, "My blood boils to think of altering one comma!"

Calm down. A good copyeditor is an invaluable aide and ally to you, as indispensable to the writer as a Sherpa guide is to someone trying to climb Mt. Everest. Trouble is, some copyeditors are not as good as they ought to be.

This problem arises more in novels than magazine fiction. Every reputable book publishing house sends your copyedited manuscript back to you. There is your precious baby, scarred and disfigured by all sorts of crazy pencil marks, littered with little stick-on notes asking embarrassing questions such as, "Why does Josephine say she loves Anthony here on page 214, when she said she hated him on page 147?"

Actually, what you are seeing now is a combination of line editing and copyediting. The line editor—often the editor who bought your novel in the first place—has the task of making your story as good as it can be. This can mean asking you to tighten the story here, straighten out an ambiguous scene there, perhaps adding some explanatory material somewhere else.

The job of the copyeditor is to make certain that your prose is grammatically and syntactically correct, except for those places where you do not want correct grammar or syntax, and that your story is internally consistent: Josephine should have blue eyes throughout the novel; they should not suddenly turn brown.

Today these two functions are sometimes blurred together. No matter who does what, you will receive your copyedited manuscript with these questions attached and all sorts of changes scribbled onto your pages.

Read every line with extreme care. A *good* copyeditor is your best friend, but all too often the copyeditor either does not understand what you are trying to achieve or — horror of horrors — the copyeditor is a frustrated writer who has decided to rewrite your manuscript the way he thinks it should have been written in the first place.

Remember, this is *your* novel. Any idiocies that appear in print will have your name on them, not the editor's or the copyeditor's. You have the right to insist that they print the words you wrote, not the copyeditor's changes. After all, that is what the editor bought, your words, your novel, not the copyeditor's version of your novel.

But with that right comes a responsibility. Make certain that you are correct: You really do want Jonathan to say "ain't" instead of "isn't"; Josephine did hate Anthony on page 147, but by page 214 she had fallen hopelessly in love with the lout. Do not get angry at the copyeditor; do not let your emotional attachment to your own words blind you to errors you have made.

I should talk. My first reaction upon looking over a copyedited manuscript is towering fury. I have learned, over the years, to put the manuscript aside for a day or so and look at it again only after I have calmed down.

However, when you see a copyeditor's "correction" that is absolutely, positively, irrevocably wrong, don't get mad: Use that fine old Latin word, *stet*. It means *let it stand*. It is your instruction to ignore the copyeditor's quibble and print the original words. Write it in red. I went out and got a stationery store to make me a rubber stamp that reads STET. It is very satisfying.

A MARKETING CHECKLIST
The following list is a review of the important points on marketing your fiction.

1. There is no way to become a published writer except to

send your manuscript to an editor at a publishing house.

2. Beware of amateur criticisms of your work. If you must have your work critiqued before sending it to market, seek professional criticism.

3. In marketing your novel, use your local bookstores to determine what category your novel fits most closely and one or more of the various writer's guides to locate the editors who regularly buy that kind of work.

4. In marketing short fiction, slant your stories to the magazines you send them to. If you do not enjoy reading a magazine, it is unlikely that you will write successfully for it.

5. Do not send your entire novel to an editor; send a query letter with sample chapters and a synopsis. For short fiction, send the entire manuscript. Always include an SASE (a self-addressed, stamped envelope).

6. You do not need an agent until a book publisher sends you a contract.

7. Manuscript preparation is important. Make your manuscript as professional-looking and easy to read as possible.

8. Good editors are a treasure—but a poor copyeditor can be infuriating.

Chapter Eighteen

The Thematic Novel

I have a theory of my own about what the art of the novel is, and how it came into being. . . . It happens because the storyteller's own experience . . . has moved him to an emotion so passionate that he can no longer keep it shut up in his heart.
— *Lady Murasaki*
  The Tale of Genji

In a sense, nobody writes about the future. Every writer is writing about the world of today and using an exotic science fiction setting as a way of showing today's problems in a more revealing light. Every writer is exorcising the demon that's tormenting him. That is why writers write and painters paint and musicians play: They are driven from within. If they were not, they would have become plumbers and lived much simpler, less stressful and wealthier lives.

There is a power in science fiction: the opportunity to *make the reader think*; the ability to reveal facets of our world through reflections from a world of imagination.

Think of the science fiction tales that have made the most lasting impression on the field. And their authors. Robert Heinlein was certainly not offering bland pastorals. Frank Herbert's *Dune* gave a major impetus to the environmental movement. Ray Bradbury showed the evil that lurks within our own hearts in those *Chronicles* about Mars, as he did in *Fahrenheit 451*. Arthur Clarke, Ursula LeGuin, Gregory Benford, Harlan Ellison — their stories have something to say far beyond the requirements of mere entertainment.

Yet the very success that science fiction has enjoyed in the marketplace has created new problems. Rank commercialism has reared its alluring head. Publishers invite writers to turn out novels based on pre-existing formats, franchised universes. Certainly one may write good fiction in a "Star Trek" format. But by using a ready-made set of characters and background, the author loses the chance to invent a unique universe and people it with fresh characters. Perhaps some writers feel that this is the best they can do. I challenge that self-defeating assumption. Dream your own dreams! Write your own stories.

SF CLICHÉS

All too often writers tend to fall back on standard backgrounds that were fresh and exciting a couple of generations ago, but have become stale and trite today. Face it, interstellar spaceships are not going to operate like ocean liners. No one will establish colonies on any of the planets of this solar system. The world will not revert to feudalism in the aftermath of a global catastrophe. When we finally meet intelligent aliens they will not be like any creature of Earth, either physically or mentally.

With all the enormities of space and time to play with, it is distressing that so few writers think any original thoughts. They tend to fall back on the well-trodden backgrounds and ideas from the stories that they read when they were young and impressionable.

My own work, for the most part, has stuck pretty close to the here-and-now. Maybe that is because I have spent so much of my life dealing with the politics of science; after all, you write best about what you know best. The juncture where science and politics meet is a fascinating area for me.

The *Voyagers* novels, for example, begin with the world as it was in the late 1970s and then examine the changes that would be caused by the certain knowledge that other intelligent races exist in the universe. What would Washington and Moscow and Beijing do if they knew that an alien spacecraft had entered the solar system? What would the Pope do? Or Billy Graham?

Turning Clichés Into New Ideas

The "invasion from space" plot is a hoary old theme, I know. I knew it when I first started writing *Voyagers*. Back in the fifties, when the hydrogen bomb and the Cold War were new and so terrifying that suburbanites were digging bomb shelters, science fiction abounded with tales in which the bickering nations of Earth united to face a threatened invasion from space. Often the threat was a phony, the work of a few brilliant scientists who wanted to unite the world and avert World War III.

In the *Voyagers* novels I took the opposite tack. It seemed obvious to me that the bickering governments would each strive their utmost to be the first to contact the incoming aliens, to make a deal that would put the aliens on their side. Even when they reluctantly agree to a joint scientific effort to contact the alien spacecraft, their secret agenda is to use the scientists to further their own chances of getting all that juicy alien technology for themselves.

Was I writing about the future? About alien contact? On the surface, yes. Actually, I was using the concept of advanced aliens as a metaphor for advanced technology. How do governments and corporations and individual persons face up to the titanic changes brought about by swiftly advancing technology? That is the real subject of the three-volume *Voyagers* tale. Nobody writes about the future.

I could give other examples. My novel *Mars* is a very realistic look at the first human expedition to the red planet. We follow the astronauts and scientists on their mission and the politicians and loved ones who remain on Earth. We see Mars as it really is, or as nearly so as possible, based on what our unmanned probes of Mars have revealed.

Beyond the surface story, *Mars* has a subtext that examines a vitally intriguing issue (at least it is intriguing to me). How do scientists gather new knowledge when they are out at the jagged edge of observability and understanding? When two scientists look at the same shaky piece of newly obtained information and see radically different things, how do they react? How do they feel? What do they say and do to prove one point of view and reject the other?

When one scientist thinks he sees a cliff dwelling set into the cleft of a Martian rift valley and the others think he's crazy, how do they settle the question? They have neither the time nor the equipment to get to the cliff for a hands-on examination. That is what *Mars* is really all about.

The point is that I try, in my novels, to offer something to think about. I try to bring fresh ideas and fresh challenges to the reader's mind.

NOVELS WITH A POINT OF VIEW

My dear friend Gordy Dickson calls such works "thematic novels," meaning novels that have a strong point of view, which the author wants to impart to the reader. Sometimes, when the author goes too far, such works can slip into propaganda. Done properly they can be powerful statements that make readers *think*. Remember Heinlein, Herbert, et al.

I believe science fiction should encourage people to think. God knows we have enough forms of amusement that discourage or actively prevent rational thought. Even in most of contemporary literature (and a growing percentage of SF), the emphasis is on emotional reaction rather than rational thought. Science fiction is the home ground for the thematic novel today; science fiction can and should be for the thinking reader.

Many of my novels begin with a theme, a point of view, an idea that I want to explore. This does not mean that I sit down to write the fictional equivalent of a political pamphlet, where I want to support a certain position that is well established in my mind before the first word is put down. I am not in the diatribe business, neither am I a partisan of any fixed political party or formula.

I regard these thematic novels as true explorations, where the author and reader investigate a certain concept or group of ideas, examine a mindset, look at a world that might actually come into being within the lifetime of the reader.

The danger of the thematic novel is that it can slide into propaganda, as noted above. There are two things that the author can (must!) do to avoid falling into this pit.

First, do your own thinking. *Never* sit down to write a story that supports an existing political position. Develop characters that represent powerfully opposing views, and let them work out their own positions as the story progresses. If all goes well, those characters will soon enough take over the story and carry it to conclusions that you, the author, were not aware of when you began writing.

Second, eschew the pleasure of creating a villain. Every story needs a protagonist and an antagonist, even if the antagonist is nature itself or the inner conflicts within the protagonist's soul. In thematic novels the antagonist tends to be a person, a character. The author must know that character so well that the novel could be turned around 180 degrees, written from the antagonist's point of view, making the villain into the hero.

As a thought experiment, imagine writing *Hamlet* from the point of view of Claudius. After all, he is the only sane person in all of Elsinore. He may be ruthless. He has certainly committed murder. Or perhaps he is merely a strong man who fell hopelessly in love with his brother's wife. Interesting possibilities there.

WHAT WOULD HAPPEN IF . . .

To make a thematic novel work well, the story should have a strong relationship to the real world. This is why I set most of my novels in the near future, the years that most readers can confidently expect to see for themselves. The world that I usually start with is the world as it exists today, or will exist in the next decade or so. Then I begin to examine what would happen if. . . .

This technique has served many writers quite well, over the years. It was H.G. Wells' standard operating procedure. (If you are going to steal, steal from the best.)

When you begin your creative work with the real world, you must then populate such stories with real people. These characters should behave as people normally do, at least at the outset of the story. They must be people whom the reader can recognize and sympathize with. Even the aliens and robots must display human emotions and human problems. Otherwise they will be too abstruse or, worse, too dull for the reader to care about.

Remember, the reader wants to be the protagonist. The true art of fiction is to sweep the reader into the world you have created and make the reader forget she is sitting in an uncomfortable chair squinting at your words in a book. The protagonist should be someone that the reader wants to be. Every work of fiction is an exercise in psychological projection.

I want to use my own double novel, *The Kinsman Saga*, as an example of what I have been talking about.

In 1966 I was working at the laboratory where the first high-power lasers were invented. I helped to arrange the first top-secret briefing in the Pentagon to show the Department of Defense that lasers were now much more than laboratory curiosities.

It became clear to those of us involved in this work that such lasers could eventually lead to a system of armed satellites in orbit capable of destroying ballistic missiles.

I examined that possibility in the novels *Millennium* and *Kinsman*. Years later, I rewrote them in the light of unfolding history and combined them into the *Kinsman Saga*.

I had no political ax to grind. When I wrote *Millennium* and *Kinsman* there was no Strategic Defense Initiative; SDI would not begin until almost ten years later. What I wanted, as an author, was to examine how the advent of this new technology would effect global politics, and the life of a certain human being whom fate casts into a pivotal role in this arena.

Chet Kinsman was a character I knew very well from short stories I had been writing over the years. He became the pivotal character for the novels. The other characters were drawn from life, including at least one friend who happens to be a well-known science fiction writer and another who is a world-famous folk singer.

The technology dictated the time frame for the novel. The characters drove the plot to its climax.

Interestingly, when the individual novels were originally published in the mid-1970s, they were reviewed very kindly. When *The Kinsman Saga* was published in 1987 — the same two novels, slightly rewritten — it was attacked on political grounds. The science fictional dream of an orbital defense against nuclear missiles had become the real-life Strategic Defense Initiative, "Star Wars," and *The Kinsman Saga* found itself in the midst of a highly politicized controversy.

RISKS OF THE THEMATIC NOVEL

Which brings us to the risks that the thematic novel presents to the author.

The first risk is that history catches up with near-future novels. Much of the *Saga* is history now, and some of it is history that never happened in the real world. By the turn of the century we will see if the technologies that are now called Star Wars lead to a more peaceful world in which no nation's missiles can threaten anyone. By then the *Saga* will have to stand on its own as literature without any prophetic overtones, just as *1984* and a myriad of first-men-to-the-Moon novels have had to face the music.

The second risk, and this surprised me, is political prejudice. As noted above, *The Kinsman Saga* was attacked by critics as hawkish, even when the story concluded with an international organization rising from the ashes of the United Nations to maintain world peace. The very same novel led some real hawks to denounce the *Saga* for its liberal, internationalist flavor! (I don't feel much like either a hawk or a dove. As an admirer of Athena, my totem is the owl.)

Those are the risks of writing thematic novels. I think that science fiction is ideally suited to such work, which is why I am in this field. It is not the gadgetry that is important. I have been called a hard-science writer for decades now, even though I have been writing about politics and sociology.

What is important is that this field of contemporary literature that we call science fiction allows a writer the scope to examine real ideas and the real world. Which in turn offers a writer the chance to say something worthwhile, to write fiction that can have an impact on readers.

Science fiction should be about something. It should make readers think. To throw away that opportunity, to sidestep that responsibility, is a criminal waste of time and talent.

William Faulkner summed it all up in his Nobel Prize speech in 1950 when he said the writer "must teach himself that the basest of all things is to be afraid and, teaching himself that, forget it forever, leaving no room in his workshop for anything but the old verities and truths of the heart, the old universal truths lacking which any story is ephemeral and doomed—love and honor and pity and pride and compassion and sacrifice."

Whether you are writing science fiction or nursery rhymes, remember that Faulkner's universal truths are the materials you should be working with.

Good luck.

Chapter Nineteen

Ideas, Style and Inspiration

The task of a writer consists in being able to make *something out of an* idea.

    —Thomas Mann

There is much more to producing good fiction than merely sitting at a desk and writing. As we have seen, a great deal of thinking and preparation must be done before you write, and some mechanical things such as typing the final manuscript and cover letter remain to be done after you have finished the story. And you must give careful thought to marketing your work, too.

But before you even begin to prepare, you must have some idea of what you intend to write about. Where do ideas come from? How do you get good ideas for your stories?

IDEAS

Probably the biggest misconception that new writers burden themselves with is the notion that ideas are rare and difficult to come by. This is especially worrisome among those who want to write science fiction, where the idea content of the stories is so important.

Yet, as any experienced writer knows, ideas are the easiest part of the job. The air is filled with ideas. Most professional writers have more ideas than time or energy to write about them.

So, where do all these story ideas come from?

Look around you. All the people you know are living with conflict, hope, ambition, love, jealousy, fear—the material for a thousand stories is at your fingertips. Look within yourself. You have hopes and hatreds, goals and passions. Every human life is a walking library of stories.

By itself, this material does not make good fiction. But it is the raw material for good stories, whether they turn out to be science fiction or soap opera. All stories are about people, and you have people surrounding you constantly. They will literally give you story ideas, if you are merely observant and patient enough.

How do you turn something that happens to you—say, an argument with a friend—into a story? There are two things to remember.

First, reduce that argument to a pair of emotional conflicts. That is, take the two people concerned and find out what their internal emotional conflicts were. Probe your own inner feelings honestly, ruthlessly. Perhaps you were torn by *pride* vs. *loyalty*, while the person you were arguing with had a conflict of *ambition* vs. *honesty*. Fine. This gives you a pair of characters, a protagonist and an antagonist, to form the central backbone of your story.

The second thing is to ask yourself a question that is fundamental to all good stories: "What if? . . ." What if these two characters had that kind of conflict while serving in the crew of a space station? And what if the subject of the argument had been something much more serious, such as whether or not to abandon the space station because its life-support system was beginning to break down?

Most good SF stories are built around that intriguing question, What if? . . . Many times a writer will begin with that question, then add people and human conflict to the basic situation to flesh out the story line.

Try a challenge. Take this basic What if? question and make a story out of it. What if someone invented a lie detector that was absolutely foolproof. The device can detect whenever a person is lying; it can even show when a person's statements are at variance with the known facts of the situation, even though the person believes he is telling the truth.

Take that idea, people it with characters you know personally, pick a protagonist who already has a powerful internal conflict that this new situation will aggravate and accentuate, and make the background—from clothing to politics—consistent with a

society that would use such an invention ruthlessly. See what happens to the criminal justice system. See what happens to ordinary people caught in the jaws of a remorseless bureaucracy.

Now another challenge. Write down three What if? situations of your own, then match each of them with a protagonist and an internal conflict. Many writers, when starting with an idea for a situation, ask themselves a different sort of question: "Whom will this hurt?"

If your What if? leads you to a scenario in which the Middle East has run out of oil, find the person who will be hurt by this and make that person the focus of your story. If your idea revolves around a new serum that allows people to become virtually immortal, find out who's going to suffer from this (there will be somebody) and make that person the focus.

Watch the human conflicts around you. That is vital for any kind of fiction writing.

Keeping Current

If you intend to write science fiction, it will also be important to stay abreast of what is happening in scientific research and technological development. You will need to know what science is doing. New ideas are always popping up and old ones are constantly revised and sometimes discarded. Just a look at the news of science this week, as I write this, includes the possibility that changes in one's diet may avert cancer; newfound data on the links between volcanic eruptions and changes in the global climate; how dolphins use sonar to communicate; two new galaxies, the most distant yet discovered, that seem unlike other galaxies in strange ways; a miniature robot designed to explore the interior of volcanoes that broke four of its eight legs on a field test.

Plenty of material for stories!

I got those items merely by leafing through this week's issue of *Science News*, which is a terrific little news magazine written for ordinary people who are interested in science. The monthly *Scientific American* requires some perseverance to read, but it is an invaluable source of detailed information in many areas of scientific research and technological development. *Discover* magazine, also monthly, offers easier reading, but less depth.

And my old alma mater, *Omni* magazine, lives up to its slogan, "The magazine of the future."

To go deeper, there are several popular astronomy magazines, including *Sky and Telescope* and the Astronomical Society of the Pacific's *Mercury*; *Science*, published weekly by the American Association for the Advancement of Science, which leans toward technical articles on biology and chemistry; and two excellent magazines published by the Smithsonian Institution, *Smithsonian* and *Air & Space*. Then there are *Natural History*, published by the New York Museum of Natural History; *Technology Review*, published by the Massachusetts Institute of Technology; and many others.

These journals are usually available at most city public libraries. If your library does not subscribe to them, the librarian can probably obtain copies for you through interlibrary loan. There are all sorts of wonderful books about science, too. Check your library and bookstores. Read and enjoy.

Juxtaposition

One final tip about ideas. If there is a single shortcut to creativity, it is the trick of juxtaposition. For example, when Galileo first heard that a Dutch maker of reading spectacles had invented a device that made distant objects appear nearby, the Italian physicist went out and made a telescope of his own, even though all he knew was that a combination of lenses was what did the trick. Legend has it he sawed off a length of church organ pipe for the barrel of his instrument.

That took a good deal of ingenuity. But the really creative thing that Galileo did was to immediately turn his telescope to the heavens, instead of seeing how many church steeples he could find with his new toy. By combining a new invention with an old interest in astronomy, Galileo ushered in the modern age of thought.

Storytellers do the same thing. In mathematics you may not be allowed to add apples and oranges, but in fiction it's always good practice to juxtapose two unlikely elements. Alfred Bester put a murderer into a future civilization where the police were telepathic in his classic *The Demolished Man*. Anne McCaffrey combined a sensitive young woman's disembodied brain with a powerful intersteller spaceship to produce "The Ship Who

Sang." Ray Bradbury brought hungry lions into a suburban nursery in his tale, "The Veldt."

Ideas are all around you. Observe carefully. Look for the underlying emotional conflicts within the people you know; those are the raw materials of stories. Study the scientific literature. Even if you have no intention of writing science fiction, it is fun and fascinating, and a treasure trove of What if? ideas. Juxtapose ideas freely. Mix and match them until you get a pair, or a set, that strikes sparks in your mind.

Then write!

A FEW WORDS ABOUT STYLE

Nathaniel Hawthorne, author of *The House of the Seven Gables* and one of America's first literary giants, once wrote:

> I am glad you think my style plain. I never, in any one page or paragraph, aimed at making it anything else. . . . The greatest possible merit of style is, of course, to make the words absolutely disappear into the thought.

I agree with Mr. Hawthorne 100 percent.

Maybe it is because I started out in the newspaper game. (It is never called a business by the workers in the field.) Or maybe because I have spent most of my adult life working with scientists and engineers. Or maybe because I care about my readers too much. Whatever the reason, I have never felt that writing should be a contest between author and reader, a battleground filled with obscurity and arcania. I do not want my readers to struggle with my prose. I do not want to impress them with how smart I am. I want them to enjoy what I am writing and maybe think a little about what I am trying to say.

The problem is, when you write clearly and simply, without stylistic frills or rococo embellishments, some people think that you are not a deep thinker or a stylist.

Isaac Asimov ran into this predicament often. Critics could not fault Isaac on his knowledge or his success, or even his earnestness or political correctness, so they belittled his style, calling it pedestrian or simplistic. Yet Isaac's style was the one thing that made him such a success, at least as far as his nonfiction work was concerned.

Other specialists knew their subjects in more depth than Isaac did. Isaac had a tremendous breadth of knowledge, but in any particular field — be it cosmology or poetry, biblical scholarship or even biochemistry — there were specialists who knew a lot more than he did.

It was Isaac's genius to be able to take any of those specialized fields and write about them so clearly, so naturalistically, that just about anyone who could read could learn the fundamentals of Isaac's subject. That took *style*! I doubt that it was totally unconscious, the work of unreflective genius. Isaac thought about what he did, every step of the way. He deliberately developed a writing style that was so deceptively unpretentious and naturalistic that critics thought what he did was easy.

In fiction, the academic disdain for straightforward, honest prose has lead critics to dismiss Hemingway and praise Faulkner, although today we are seeing that Hemingway's work is standing the test of time better than his contemporaries'. Maybe Hemingway was also influenced by his early days of newspapering. We know that he deliberately developed the lean, understated style that became his hallmark. He worked hard at it, every year of his writing life.

It seems strange when you stop to think about it, but most science fiction stories are written in a very naturalistic, realistic style. Fantastic settings and incredible feats may abound in such stories, yet the prose is usually unadorned and straightforward. There is a reason for this. If you want to make the reader believe what you are saying, if you want the reader to accept those fantastic backgrounds and incredible deeds, it is easier if the prose you use is as simple and realistic as you can make it.

Again, look at H.G. Wells. In almost journalistic prose he can take us from a Victorian drawing room to a time-travel adventure or an invasion from Mars. He gets us to accept the ordinary setting that he starts with, then carries us along into a fantastic tale.

Experimental writing is no stranger to science fiction, and several of the best SF writers are known more for their style than their content. But in general, hard science fiction is presented in realistic prose so that the reader can forget about the writing style and concentrate on the story. The prose style becomes transparent, like a looking glass that we step through to get into the marvelous world on its other side.

The writing style helps to get the reader to suspend disbelief and accept the reality of the tale being told. However, the story must be consistent, otherwise the reader stops suspending his disbelief. It is perfectly possible to lead the reader from the here-and-now to the mines on the Moon or the cloning of the President of the United States or the struggles of a religious sect to establish a colony on the planet of another star. But it must be done in a way that does not jar the reader so badly that he stops reading.

In my own work I have tried to keep the prose clean and clear, especially when I am writing about subjects as complex as space exploration, politics and love. Those subjects are tricky enough without trying to write about them in convoluted sentences heavy with opaque metaphors and intricate similes.

Then, there is the difference between the optimists and the pessimists. Somehow, somewhere in the course of time, darkly pessimistic stories got to be considered more literary than brightly optimistic ones. I suspect this attitude began in academia, although it is a rather juvenile perspective: Teenagers frequently see the world they face as too big and complex, too awesome for them to fathom. Healthy adults saw off a chunk of that world for themselves and do their best to cultivate it. That is the message of Voltaire's *Candide*, after all.

Even within the SF field, pessimistic, downbeat stories are regarded as intrinsically more sophisticated than optimistic, upbeat tales. I suspect this reveals a hidden yearning within the breasts of some SF people to be accepted by the academic/literary establishment. That is a legitimate goal, I suppose, but such yearnings should not cloud our perceptions.

It may be de rigueur in academic circles to moan about the myth of Sisyphus and the pointless futility of human existence, but such an attitude is antithetical to the principles of science fiction. Science fiction, like science itself, is fundamentally optimistic. It is based on the premise that rational human thought can understand the universe. Science fiction people tend to see the human race not as failed angels but as apes struggling toward godhood. Even in the darkest dystopian science fiction stories, there is hope for the future. This is the literature that can take up a situation such as the Sun blowing up and ask, "Okay, what happens next?" (If you don't believe me, read Larry Niven's

"Inconstant Moon" or my own *Test of Fire*.)

Does that make science fiction silly? Or pedestrian? Or juvenile? Not at all. In science fiction we deal with the real world and try to honestly examine where in the universe we are and where we are capable of going.

In good science fiction, that is. Remember Sturgeon's Law. All that bears the title science fiction is not in Ted's top 5 percent. But at its best, science fiction tends to be optimistic.

Yet academic critics often regard science fiction as simplistic or lacking style or less literary than other forms of contemporary literature. Such complaints are the price to be paid for writing simply and basing fiction on the real world and actual human behavior.

Take my novel *Mars*, for example. It deals as realistically as possible with the first human expedition to the planet Mars. The writing style is straightforward and realistic, except where I want to weave in portions of Navaho myth to serve as a counterpoint. Then the style is rather different.

Is the novel simplistic? It deals with several dozen characters from almost as many nations, some of them scientists, some astronauts or cosmonauts, some politicians and government bureaucrats. It deals with the way national governments handle major scientific projects and how the scientists work their own inner politics. It deals with the way the news media cover Big Science. Above all, it deals with a man who is torn between the Navaho and the Anglo, the Earth and its brotherworld Mars.

There are many levels to the novel, but I deliberately refrained from writing it in a style that called attention to this depth. I do not like watching actors who are working so hard you are aware that they are acting. And I do not like reading novels so filled with self-conscious references and citations that you are aware of the author's presence on every page.

For example, here is a description of what the protagonist of the novel, Jamie Waterman, experiences on his first night on the surface of Mars. The team of explorers has put up a pressurized dome that will be their base while they explore the planet. It has been a busy day for the explorers, exhausting both physically and mentally.

Feeling completely spent, Jamie tumbled onto his cot

without bothering to undress. Nearly an hour later he still lay awake on the spindly cot in his cubicle. . . . The dome was dark now, but not silent. The metal and plastic creaked and groaned as the cold of the Martian night tightened its grip. Pumps were chugging softly and air fans humming. The psychologists had decided that such noises would actually be comforting to the lonely explorers. . . .

As he lay on his cot, though, Jamie heard another sound. A rhythmic sort of sighing that came and went, started and stopped. A low whispering, almost like a soft moaning, so faint that Jamie at first thought it was imagination. But it persisted, a strange ghostly breathing just barely audible over the background chatter of the man-made equipment.

The wind.

There was a breeze blowing softly across their dome, stroking this new alien artifact with its gentle fingers. Mars was caressing them, the way a child might reach out to touch something new and inexplicable. Mars was welcoming them gently.

Plain, unadorned style. But the concepts expressed in that style are far from simple or pedestrian.

There are other complexities to *Mars*. The novel skips around in time. One clock is set for the actual mission on the Martian surface. In fact, the novel begins (after a brief prologue) with the first lander touching down on the rust-red sands of Mars. But there are extensive flashbacks to show the training and crew selection and political jockeying that took place before the mission left Earth. And even during the mission the scenes shift back and forth between Mars and Houston, Washington, New York, Rio de Janeiro, Moscow.

Of necessity, *Mars* deals with high technology. But again, I wanted the reader to live with the characters, not to be stunned by how much I know about the way a spacecraft works. So the high-tech is there as transparently as possible, just the way the characters themselves would think of it. As normal as buttoning a shirt. No, "Look, Ma! I'm fradgerating the ampersand!"

Simplistic, *Mars* is not. Does the writing lack style? No. There is a deliberate style; in fact, a deliberate mix of styles, throughout the novel. You may not *like* the style. You may think the style is poor. That is your decision to make. But to those critics who commented that there was not enough style in the prose, I say (like Mr. Hawthorne), "Thank you! That is precisely what I was trying to achieve."

INSPIRATION AND PERSPIRATION

Thomas Edison said, "Success is made up of 1 percent inspiration and 99 percent perspiration." The simple fact is, that is quite true.

All the studying, thinking, idea-generating, talking and planning in the world are not going to get a single word down on paper. In the end, it is those long, lonely hours when there is nothing in the universe except you and your writing instrument that will determine how successful a writer you will be.

It would be easy to wax poetic at this point and try to fill you with enthusiasm and esprit de corps about the wonderful profession of writing. Truth is, it's as much work as digging ditches, and the most emotionally demanding profession I know. The average writer's income from writing is far below the government's official poverty line.

As a writer you are always putting your guts on paper, allowing editors, critics and readers to take free kicks at you. Isaac Asimov once pointed out that he could read a review of his latest book that consisted of five thousand words of closely reasoned praise and one tiny sentence of mild criticism. It was that one sentence that kept him awake all night. Irwin Shaw said, "An absolutely necessary part of a writer's equipment, almost as necessary as talent, is the ability to stand up under punishment, both the punishment the world hands out and the punishment he inflicts upon himself."

Writing is hard and lonely work. The hazards and pains, especially at the beginning, far outweigh the rewards. And yet . . . and yet. . . .

Many years ago, the United Nations published a book of pictures by the greatest photographers in the world called *The Faces of Man*.

One of these photographs has always stuck in my mind. It shows an African village, where everybody has gathered around an old, withered man who is evidently the village storyteller. He is at a high point in the evening's story; his arms are raised over his head, his mouth is agape, his eyes wide. And the whole village is staring at him, equally agape and wide-eyed, breathless to find out what happens next.

That is what storytelling is all about.

There is no older, more honored, more demanding, more frustrating, more satisfying or rewarding profession in the universe. If the only thing that separates us from the beasts is our intelligence and our ability to speak, then storytelling is the most uniquely human activity there can be.

I waxed poetic after all, didn't I?

BIBLIOGRAPHY

Asimov, Isaac, ed. *The Hugo Winners*. Vol. 1. New York: Doubleday, 1969. Reprint. New York: Fawcett, 1977. Vol. 2. New York: Doubleday, 1971. Vol. 3. New York: Doubleday, 1977. Reprint. New York: Fawcett, 1979.

Bova, Ben, ed. *Science Fiction Hall of Fame*. Vol. 2a and 2b. New York: Doubleday, 1973. Reprint. New York: Avon, 1974.

Bova, Ben, ed. *The Best of the Nebulas*. New York: T. Doherty, Tor Books, 1989.

Card, Orson Scott. *How to Write Science Fiction and Fantasy*, edited by Nan Dibble. Cincinnati: Writer's Digest Books, 1990.

Carr, Robyn. *Practical Tips for Writing Popular Fiction*. Cincinnati: Writer's Digest Books, 1992.

De Camp, L. Sprague, and Catherine C. De Camp. *Science Fiction Handbook, Revised*. Philadelphia: Owlswick Press, 1975.

Foster-Harris, William. *The Basic Formulas of Fiction*. Rev. ed. Norman: University of Oklahoma Press, 1967.

Graves, Robert, and Alan Hodge. *The Reader Over Your Shoulder*. 2d ed., rev. New York: Random House, 1979.

Gunn, James E. *Alternate Worlds: The Illustrated History of Science Fiction*. Englewood Cliffs, N.J.: Prentice-Hall, 1975.

McKenna, Richard. *New Eyes for Old: Nonfiction Writings*. Edited by Eva Grice McKenna and Shirley Graves Cochrane. Winston-Salem, N.C.: John F. Blair, 1972.

Ochoa, George, and Jeffrey Osier. *The Writer's Guide to Creating a Science Fiction Universe*. Cincinnati: Writer's Digest Books, 1993.

Silverberg, Robert, ed. *Science Fiction Hall of Fame*. Vol. 1. Garden City, N.Y.: Doubleday, 1970. Reprint. New York: Avon, 1971.

Twain, Mark. "Fenimore Cooper's Literary Offenses." In *The Portable Mark Twain*, edited by Bernard De Voto. New York: Viking, 1968.

Williamson, J.N., ed. *How to Write Tales of Horror, Fantasy and Science Fiction*. Cincinnati: Writer's Digest Books, 1987.

Several anthologies of SF stories are published each year. Also, the Science-fiction and Fantasy Writers of America produce a Nebula Award anthology each year, titled *The Nebula Awards*.

The definitive news magazine of science fiction is *Locus*, published by Charles Brown, Locus Publications, Box 13305, Oakland CA 94661.

INDEX

Action, 109, 146; of characters, 113; off stage, 74-75; physical, 80-81, 102
Advance, 149
Agents, 189-192
Air & Space, 208
Alien, 80-81
Analog Science Fiction-Science Fact, 2, 3, 7, 188
Antagonist, 83, 155, 201-02; nonhuman, 86, 141, 142, 155
Anticlimax, 144
Asimov, Isaac, 6, 7, 43, 48, 105, 106, 164, 186, 209-10, 214
Astronomical Society of the Pacific, 208
Audience, 18, 188

Background, 4, 146, 176; checklist for, 51; consistency in, 49-50, 78; drawn from life, 46; information, 110-11; overwritten, 42-43; practice in, 72-78; purposes for, 73; in sciences, 45-47; theory of, 41-51
Benford, Gregory, 198
Book publishers, and subsidiary rights, 190-91
Bradbury, Ray, 9, 34, 43, 47, 109, 198

Campbell, John W., 2, 8
Card, Orson Scott, 42, 184
Category fiction, 185-86
Chain of problems, 35-36, 86, 103, 146
Change, as story element, 38, 40, 112-13
Chapters, endings, 173; outline, 156-57
Character sketches, 151-52
Characters, 8, 9-10, 14, 16, 154-55, 202; actions of, 146; and chart of appearances, 153-54; checklist for, 19-20, 38-39; and conflict, 13-15; minor, 34, 175-76; practice in, 34-40; and surprises, 108-09; theory of, 12-20; types of, 12
Clarke, Author C., 48, 76, 105, 198
Clichés, 44, 199-200
Cliff hanger, 173
Climax, 113, 145, 146, 156
Cold War, 34, 199-200
Colony, 153, 167-69, 171
Complications, 156
Composite characters, 160
Compounding, 169
Computers, 151, 180, 193
Conflict, 4, 9-10, 12, 74, 86, 100, 101, 102-03, 155; and characters, 13-15; checklist for, 86, 102; defined, 80, 81-83; emotional, 14, 15, 34; levels of, 81, 83-86; and plot, 106; practice in, 99-103; theory of, 79-87
Conrad, Joseph, 173, 176
Consistency, 49
Contracts, 191

Cover letters, 194-95
"Crisis of the Month," 105, 106; analysis of, 99-103; complete story, 88-98; development, 99-100; and plot, 141
Crisis-point, 36-38
Criticism, 183-84

Decision-point, 36-38
Desk book, 151-54, 162
Details, 44-45, 75-76, 153
Dialect, 175
Dialogue, 109, 110, 174-75
Dickens, Charles, 50, 158
Dilemma, 36
Dr. Jekyll and Mr. Hyde, 82-83
Dr. Strangelove, 104
Dune, 104

Edison, Thomas, 214
Editors, 184-85, 192-93, 195-96
Ellison, Harlan, 9, 107, 163, 198
Employment, and writing, 2
Ender's Game, 42
Endings, 36-37, 109, 113, 173
Episodic novel, 158-59

Fahrenheit 451, 198
Faulkner, William, 165-66, 204, 210
"Fifteen Miles," 73, 86, 105; analysis of, 34-40; background of, 18-19; complete story, 21-33; and plot, 141
First draft, 150, 179
First person, 17, 167
Fitzgerald, F. Scott, 104, 170
Flashbacks, 174
Formula for conflict, 14, 37, 82, 83, 84, 206
Frankenstein, 6

Gimmick stories, 106

Haldeman, Joe, 107, 184
Hamlet, 14, 157, 202
Hawthorne, Nathaniel, 209, 214
Heinlien, Robert A., 37, 198, 201
Hemingway, Ernest, 1, 41, 159, 175, 179, 210
Herbert, Frank, 104, 201
Homer, 5, 75, 102, 172
Horse opera, 80

Ideas, 3, 7-8, 205-07
Invention, of devices, 45-46, 76-77

James, Henry, 12, 145
Jargon, 43-44

Kinsman Saga, The, 156, 202, 203, 204
Komroff, Manuel, 35-36
Kubrick, Stanley, 76, 104

LeGuin, Ursula, 198

PLEASE!

DO NOT REMOVE
THE DATE DUE CARD
FROM THIS POCKET.

THERE IS A $1.00
FINE IF YOU LOSE IT!

Marlborough Public Library
Marlborough, Mass.

RULES